W9-CDB-481

Low-Wage Employment in Europe

Low-Wage Employment in Europe

Edited by

Stephen Bazen,

LARE, Université Montesquieu

Bordeaux France

Mary Gregory

St Hilda's College, Oxford University
Oxford, UK

Wiemer Salverda

Faculty of Economics, University of Groningen
Groningen, the Netherlands

European Low-Wage Employment Research Network (LoWER)

Edward Elgar
Cheltenham, UK • Northampton, MA, USA

© Stephen Bazen, Mary Gregory and Wiemer Salverda 1998

All rights reserved. No part of this publication may be reproduced, stored in a retrieval system or transmitted in any form or by any means, electronic, mechanical or photocopying, recording, or otherwise without the prior permission of the publisher.

Published by
Edward Elgar Publishing Limited
Glensanda House
Montpellier Parade
Cheltenham
Glos GL50 1UA
UK

Edward Elgar Publishing, Inc.
6 Market Street
Northampton
Massachusetts 01060
USA

3 2280 00609 0799

A catalogue record for this book
is available from the British Library

Library of Congress Cataloguing in Publication Data

Low-wage employment in Europe / edited by Stephen Bazen, Mary Gregory,
    Wiemer Salverda
        Papers presented at a conference, Université Montesquieu Bordeaux IV.
        1. Wages—Europe—Congresses. 2. Full employment policies–
    –Europe—Congresses. 3. Minimum wage—Europe—Congresses.
    I. Bazen, Stephen. II. Gregory, Mary. III. Salverda, Wiemer.
    HD5014.L693   1999
    331.2'94—dc21   98–27888
                                                              CIP

ISBN 1 85898 932 9

Printed and bound in Great Britain by
Biddles Ltd, Guildford and King's Lynn

Contents

PART THREE
LOW PAY AMONG SCHOOL-LEAVERS

Figures

Tables

List of Contributors

Didier Balsan, Ecole des Hautes Etudes en Sciences Sociales, Marseille, France

Stephen Bazen, LARE, Université Montesquieu Bordeaux IV, France

Holger Buch, University of Göttingen, Germany

Juan J. Dolado, Universidad Carlos III, Madrid, Spain

Florentino Felgueroso, Universidad de Oviedo, Spain

Mary Gregory, St. Hilda's College, University of Oxford, UK

Saïd Hanchane, Centre d'Etudes et de Recherches sur l'Emploi et les Qualifications, Marseille, France

Juan F. Jimeno, Universidad de Alcala de Henares, Spain

Ive Marx, Centre for Social Policy, University of Antwerp, Belgium

Brian Nolan, Economic and Social Research Institute, Dublin, Ireland

Peter Rühmann, University of Göttingen, Germany

Wiemer Salverda, University of Groningen, the Netherlands

Wendy Smits, Research Centre for Education and the Labour Market, University of Maastricht, the Netherlands

Gerre Verbist, Centre for Social Policy, University of Antwerp, Belgium

Patrick Werquin, Centre d'Etudes et de Recherches sur l'Emploi et les Qualifications, Marseille, France

Ed Willems, Research Centre for Education and the Labour Market, University of Maastricht, the Netherlands

Preface

The contributions presented in this book were initially presented at a conference on Problems of Low-wage Employment, at the Université Montesquieu Bordeaux IV. The conference was organised as part of the activities of the Low-wage Employment Research (LoWER) network financed by the European Union as part of its Targeted Socio-economic Research programme. We are grateful to the European Union for financing the work of the network, which included this conference, and to the Université Montesquieu Bordeaux IV for additonal financial support for this conference. The views expressed in this volume are those of the individaul authors and not those of the European Commission or the editors of the volume. We are very grateful to Sandrine Robert, Jessica Bakker, Alette Schippers and Suzan van Essen for help in preparing the mansucript.

1. Editors' Introduction

Stephen Bazen, Mary Gregory and Wiemer Salverda

There has been growing interest in the development of low-wage employment in Europe in the last twenty years. This has firstly been due to the prospect of reducing unemployment through the creation of large numbers of low-paid, low-skill jobs - an approach which appears to have worked in the United States (and to a lesser extent in the United Kingdom). Secondly, there has been increasing concern about the emergence in world markets of countries which are capable of producing low skill-intensive goods at a fraction of the cost of European countries. While this phenomenon at present concerns only a small proportion of total world production and is in the main limited to the manufacturing sector, pressure has been brought to bear on institutional mechanisms that prevail in the majority of European countries to regulate the low-wage labour market.

At the same time, these moves toward developing low-wage employment as an appropriate response to the problem of high and persistent unemployment, and competing with low-cost producers, have been accompanied by increasing inequality in terms of earnings and income, and increasing concern about social exclusion. Poverty has increased noticeably in the United States and the United Kingdom, and there is pressure of social welfare expenditures in a number of countries.

However, there is an ongoing debate concerning the efficacy and social desirability of the different approaches to low-wage employment. Where it is seen as a necessary development in the context of bringing down unemployment or competing in world markets, the so-called European model of social protection is called into question. Institutional mechanisms to regulate low wages - such as minimum wage legislation and collective bargaining - are regarded as harmful rather than beneficial. The protection of workers and more generally the way in which health and social security benefits are financed are seen as constraints on the creation of employment. The implication of this solution to the economic woes of Europe is that the increases in inequality and social exclusion are necessary prices to pay.

Research into the nature and consequences of low-wage employment on a European basis is a relatively recent development. The European Commission established a group of experts to examine low pay in Europe as a basis for an opinion on the concept of equitable wages. It emerged that there were a number of differences in the availability and form of sources of earnings statistics as well as more obvious institutional differences (see CERC, 1991). Nevertheless, a number of common features of low-wage employment emerged in terms of the groups of workers and activities affected. Yet there remain a number of important differences in terms of the evolution of low wage employment, its form and the role of mechanisms to regulate low wages. It is these differences that this book addresses.

The various contributions highlight particular features of the market for low-wage labour, and fall into three main groups. Firstly, there is an attempt to document and account for the evolution of low-wage employment in a comparative fashion - among European countries, and between Europe and the United States. Secondly, there are accounts of what has happened in particular countries in terms of the impact of low-wage employment on poverty, the development of new forms of low-wage employment and the role of minimum wages. Thirdly, there are analyses of the impact on young persons, who in many countries are bearing the main burden of the development of low-wage employment.

A number of interesting and sometimes unexpected conclusions emerge. Firstly, the evolution of low-wage employment is not that similar among European countries, and in certain countries it is not dissimilar to what has been experienced in the United States. Secondly, minimum wage legislation does provide protection for the lowest paid but it will not prevent the emergence of low-wage employment in the wider sense without other conditions being met. Essentially, this requires an active policy of uprating the minimum wage, that the minimum wage be the cornerstone of a more general system of wage regulation (such as a widespread system of collective bargaining) and that the minimum wage should have no significant effects on the employment of those workers it is intended to help. Thirdly, countries with highly regulated labour markets such as France and Germany have seen the development of new forms of low-wage employment which exist outside of the conventional labour market.

Research into the nature and causes of low-wage employment in Europe is an ongoing process. The work presented in the current volume represents only the first stage of a wider programme of research into the link between low wages and social exclusion.[1] At the same time, the European Commission has decided to prepare harmonised data sources on earnings and households, and this will enable deeper analysis when they become available. The current volume not only contains very useful information and analysis on the basis of existing national data sources, but also defines a number of interesting areas for future research using comparable data when these become available.

NOTE

1   The Low-Wage Employment Research (LoWER) network will organise two further conferences devoted to the analysis of the causes of low wages (London, December 1997) and on policy measures for low-wage employment (Groningen, November 1998, respectively.

REFERENCE

Centre d'Etudes sur le Revenu et les Coûts (CERC) (1991), *Les bas salaires dans les pays membres la Communauté Européenne*, La Documentation Francaise, No. 101, Paris.

PART ONE

International Comparisons

2. Low-Paid Employment in France, Great Britain and the Netherlands

Stephen Bazen, Mary Gregory and Wiemer Salverda

The issue of low-paid employment has undergone a change of emphasis in the last twenty years. Initially seen as a indicator of the effectiveness of mechanisms such as collective bargaining to regulate wages, it has since become a key issue in the debate about how Europe should deal with its ongoing unemployment problems. Essentially, the debate has shifted from concern over the social and economic consequences of the existence of high proportions of low-paid workers, towards the question of to what extent the development of low-wage employment is an acceptable approach to employment creation. This in turn has raised the question of whether protecting the low paid through institutional wage regulation mechanisms, such as minimum wages, hinders job creation of this kind. A number of European countries have already decided to pursue the low-wage option while others have done so implicitly by permitting the development of non-conventional forms of employment.

In policy terms the European experience has varied from the drive for maximum flexibility in the UK to the refusal of the low-wage approach in France. However, in between these two polar approaches lie others such as that adopted in the Netherlands, where wage regulation mechanisms have been interfered with in an attempt to increase employment. In this chapter we consider the experiences of these three countries – France, the Netherlands and the United Kingdom – which have adopted different policy stances on low wage employment. In the first section we examine how low-paid employment has evolved in each country for the period spanning the mid-1970s to the early 1990s. We then go on to account for the experience of each country, and we place particular emphasis on the role played by minimum wage legislation and other institutional factors. In the final section we set out the current policy stances of these countries, noting the shifts in position compared to the 1980s.

1   WHAT HAS HAPPENED TO LOW-WAGE EMPLOYMENT?

Defining Low Pay

In order to examine the evolution of low paid employment over time we need to define what we mean by low pay. In making international comparisons, the adoption of an absolute definition of low pay – such as 3 ECUs an hour – would normally mean that low-wage employment would not exist in richer countries of Northern Europe. Apart from differences in living costs, an absolute definition takes no account of how rich the country is, and it does not take into account the notion that certain groups of workers may not share the benefits of economic growth. A relative definition – in which a wage is deemed low in relation to the general level of wages that prevails in a country – provides a more satisfactory basis on which to make international comparisons.

In this chapter, following the work of the European Commission Working Group on Equitable Wages (as published in CERC, 1991) we adopt in each country a low-pay benchmark of two thirds of the overall level of median earnings for full-time workers. While the choice of benchmark is to a large extent arbitrary, the two thirds of the median cut-off is commonly used for two principal reasons. Firstly, in countries that have a national legal minimum wage, the level is usually such that no full-time workers earn below a benchmark of half median earnings. Secondly, a higher figure serves to emphasize that low-paid employment is not simply a matter related to the fixing of minimum wages.

Data Sources

For each country, we use earnings data from published tabulations. In order to make comparisons, we had to restrict the analysis to full-time adult workers. The exclusion of the very young and part-time workers is an unfortunate limitation in the analysis of low-wage employment given the importance of these two groups in the low-paid population. Furthermore, part-time work has played a key role in recent increases in employment both in the UK and in the Netherlands. The data we use are taken from the following employer-based surveys: the New Earnings Survey for Great Britain, the Declaration Annuelles des Données Sociales for France and the Yearly Earnings Survey for the Netherlands. The earnings definitions vary between countries as does the coverage of the survey (see Table 2.1), so that inter-country comparisons of the extent of low-paid employment are made difficult (see Atkinson and Bazen, 1984, for an attempt to compare earnings in France and Great Britain). However, our aim is to see how low-paid employment varies for each country over time, and we believe that the change over time can be reliably compared across the three countries. Chart 2.1 provides a justification for this claim.

Table 2.1:
Main features of the earnings survey data used

Country	Earnings definition	Coverage	Main exclusions
France	Annual earnings net of social security of full-time workers aged 16 to 65	Private and semi-public sectors	Civil servants, agricultural workers
Great Britain	Weekly earnings of full-time workers paid adult rates in April of each year	All sectors	Certain part-time workers, recent job- changers
The Netherlands	Weekly up to 1986 Annual after 1986	All sectors	Recent job- changers

* The entries refer to the data used here or data released into the public domain by the data collection agency. The actual data collected may not have the properties mentioned here.

Figure 2.1
Comparisons of the extent of low-paid employment

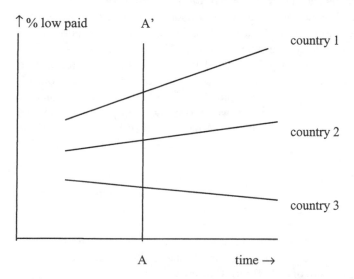

Comparisons at a given point in time place countries on a scale indicated by a vertical line such as AA'. The coverage of the earnings survey and the definition of earnings, and not simply the extent of low-wage employment, will play a crucial role in determining the position occupied by the different countries to such a degree that the ranking may be spurious. However, the direction in which low-wage employment evolves within a country is comparable across countries unless the coverage of the earnings survey is altered. A change in the structure of the labour force (e.g. more female workers) will alter the position of the median and thus the low-pay benchmark, as will a rise in unemployment (see Salverda, 1996 for an analysis of the earnings distribution in the Netherlands taking account of these kinds of changes). Nevertheless, our prime interest is whether the extent of low-wage employment has changed for whatever reason, and this can be analysed satisfactorily with the available data.

Trends in Low-Wage Employment

In order to examine in a comparative fashion how low-wage employment has evolved over time, we present a sequence of four graphs for the incidence of low-wage employment and separately for a number of earnings inequality measures. The first graph contains the country trends super-imposed one upon the other so that the overall picture can be assessed. The three others present the trends separately for each country in order to see more clearly what has happened.

In Figure 2.1, the proportion of full-time adult workers earning less than the chosen low benchmark is presented for the period 1976 to the early 1990s. The overall trends are clear-cut. In France the proportion of low-paid workers has decreased from 17% to 14%; in the UK the proportion has increased substantially from around 14% in 1977 to 20% in the mid-1990s; and in the Netherlands the proportion fell up to 1984 and increased a little thereafter. In France and the UK the trends are more or less monotonic once it is recalled that the data have at times been interpolated from published tabulations. The ranking of countries, which is not without problems, puts the UK highest in terms of the extent of low pay, followed by France with the Netherlands having the lowest proportion of low-paid workers. This ranking holds for all of the period bar the late 1970s.

The trend in low-paid employment is mirrored to a large extent in the evolution of the lowest decile wage relative to median earnings (see Figure 2.2). In the UK lowest decile earnings have declined by twelve percentage points in the period, from around 67% to 55% of median earnings. In France the lowest decile rose up to 1984 to around 62% before dropping back and stabilizing at a higher level (60%) than in the late 1970s. In the Netherlands, it varies around a figure of 64% for most of the period.

Thus the relative position of the low paid in the Netherlands and France has remained stable and has possibly slightly improved over the period considered. In the UK, it has deteriorated substantially. However, the UK has also differed in terms of the overall distribution of earnings. The ratio of the highest decile to the lowest decile of the earnings distribution has also grown substantially – from 2.4 to nearly 3.4 (see Figure 2.3). In France and the Netherlands, this ratio declined slightly over the period as a whole with the main part occurring in the period up to 1983/4. While the ratio picked up thereafter, it did not return to previous levels.

What is striking about the UK experience is that at the beginning of the period considered (the late 1970s) the ratio was at its lowest in the UK, slightly below the Netherlands and some ten points lower than in France, which exhibits a high degree of earnings inequality with a ratio of 3.4. By the early 1990s, the UK had a ratio slightly above the ratio in France. Inequality (thus measured) had fallen slightly from a high level in France, remained fairly stable and fell slightly from a low level in the Netherlands and became far more pronounced in the UK.

This rise in inequality is not simply the result of a worsening of the position of the low paid in the UK. As Figure 2.4 shows, the highest decile relative to median earnings has also risen from under 1.6 to over 1.8 over the period. In France and the Netherlands, overall there has been little net change over the period (although the ratio did fall slightly up to 1983/4 and then rise again). In the Netherlands the relative decline of the highest decile is partly the result of reductions in public sector pay during the early 1980s and the result of budget cuts. In fact public sector wage rates followed exactly the same path as the minimum wage over this period which was decreased in nominal terms and thereafter frozen (see below).

In order to see how the low paid have fared in absolute terms, in Figure 2.5 the evolution of the real value of the lowest decile wage is presented. In France there has been more or less continuous growth, while in the Netherlands it fell in the early part of the period but rose subsequently to finish at roughly the same value in real terms in the early 1990s as in the late 1970s. In the UK, the lowest decile hardly changed at all in real terms during the 1980s although there is some growth in the 1990s.

The overall picture that emerges is one where there are pressures that serve to widen the earnings distribution in all three countries. It would appear that the earnings distribution widened slightly from 1984 onwards in France and the Netherlands in response to these pressures. There was less inequality in the early 1990s compared to the late 1970s in these countries. This was mainly the result of the lowest decile not declining. On the other hand the earnings distribution widened from 1981 onwards in the UK at both ends. The lowest decile fell away and the highest decile grew slowly but monotonically relative to median earnings.

Figure 2.1a
Proportion of workers earning less than 2/3 of median earnings

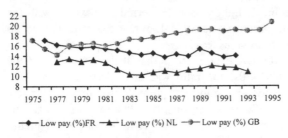

Figure 2.1b
Proportion of workers earning less than 2/3 of median earnings (%) GB

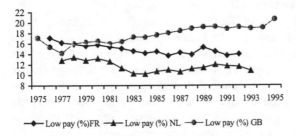

Figure 2.1c
Proportion of workers earning less than 2/3 of median earnings (%) FR

Figure 2.1d
Proportion of workers earning less than 2/3 of median earnings (%) NL

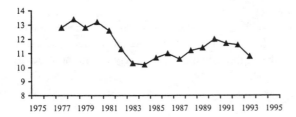

Figure 2.2a
Lowest decile relative to median earnings (%)

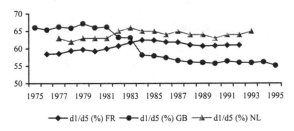

Figure 2.2b
Lowest decile relative to median earnings (%) GB

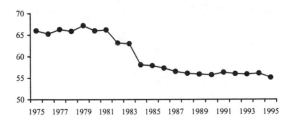

Figure 2.2c
Lowest decile relative to median earnings (%) FR

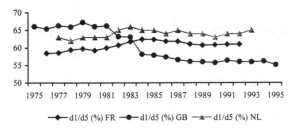

Figure 2.2d
Lowest decile relative to median earnings (%) NL

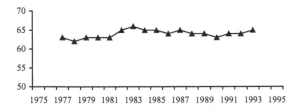

Figure 2.3a
Highest decile relative to lowest decile

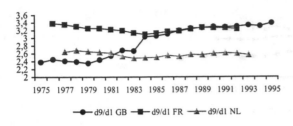

—●— d9/d1 GB —■— d9/d1 FR —▲— d9/d1 NL

Figure 2.3b
Highest decile relative to lowest decile GB

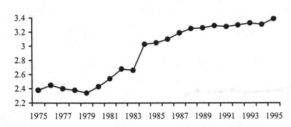

Figure 2.3c
Highest decile relative to lowest decile NL

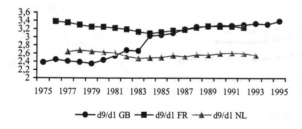

—●— d9/d1 GB —■— d9/d1 FR —▲— d9/d1 NL

Figure 2.3d
Highest decile relative to lowest decile FR

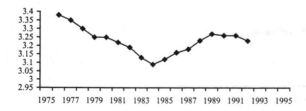

Figure 2.4a
Highest decile relative to median earnings

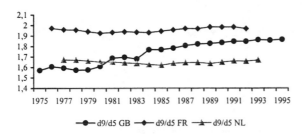

Figure 2.4b
Highest decile relative to median earning FR

Figure 2.4c
Highest decile relative to median earnings NL

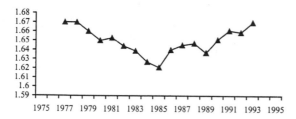

Figure 2.4d
Highest decile relative to median earnings GB

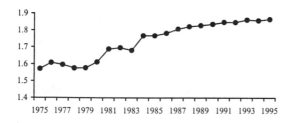

Figure 2.5a
Lowest decile in constant prices (1980 =100)

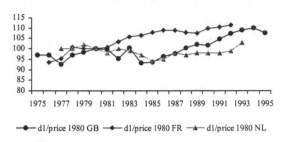

—●—d1/price 1980 GB —◆—d1/price 1980 FR —▲—d1/price 1980 NL

Figure 2.5b
Lowest decile in constant prices (1980 = 100) NL

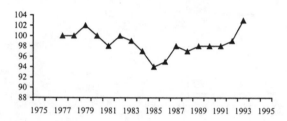

Figure 2.5c
Lowest decile in constant prices (1980 =100) GB

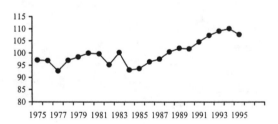

Figure 2.5d
Lowest decile in constant prices (1980 = 100) FR

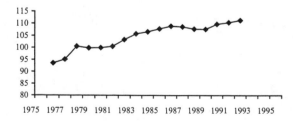

2 THE ROLE OF MINIMUM WAGES

As has already been noted, part of the explanation for differences in the observed trends in low-wage employment is the existence of institutional mechanisms to regulate low wages. Given the striking differences in how the earnings distribution has changed between the UK on the one hand and France and the Netherlands on the other, an obvious contributory factor would be the presence of national minimum wages in the latter two countries and the piecemeal, limited minimum wage protection provided by the Wages Councils in Great Britain up to 1993. In this section, we consider firstly the conditions in which a minimum wage reduces low-wage employment, secondly the attitudes of the three countries towards minimum wages and finally the impact that minimum wages have had on low wages both in real and relative terms.

Minimum Wages and Low-Wage Employment

The presence of a national minimum wage in principle provides a floor to earnings. In practice, there may be groups of workers who are excluded, and legally earn below the minimum wage. Furthermore, given the definitions of earnings used and the coverage of earnings surveys, the minimum wage will only directly affect a small minority of the workers considered. In terms of the impact of the minimum wage on the evolution of low-paid employment, two further factors will be important: the uprating policy adopted and the interaction of the minimum wage with the system of collective bargaining.

If the minimum wage is not uprated on a regular basis, the proportion affected by it will tend to fall as the rise in the general level of wages lifts them off the minimum wage. However, the relative position of someone on the minimum wage will decline, and the extent of low-wage employment will in general increase. This is what happened in the United States in the 1980s. In order to protect the relative position of the lowest paid workers, the minimum will need to rise in line with the general level of wages.

Each time the minimum wage is increased, wage differentials are initially compressed. Among the affected group of workers, differentials are eliminated: all those earning the old minimum wage, and those with earnings between the old and new minimum wage, will move up to the new value of the minimum wage. Furthermore, the gap between the minimum wage and the lowest collectively agreed rates is initially reduced. Thus each uprating brings more workers into the scope of the minimum wage and will probably trigger the renegotiation of collectively agreed wage scales. The more active the uprating policy, the greater the likelihood of the minimum wage leading to the alteration of collective agreements. Thus in order to have a real impact of the proportion of workers regarded as low paid, the minimum wage must lead to the revaluation of other rates of pay.

Minimum Wage Fixing Arrangements

One of the major differences between the three countries concerns attitudes towards minimum wages. Historically, the trade union movement in the United Kingdom has been against minimum wage legislation and has argued for wage regulation through voluntary collective bargaining. Under the Wages Councils, which fixed legally binding minimum rates in a limited number of sectors up to 1993, a number were in fact abolished due to the development of satisfactory collective bargaining arrangements (see Craig, Rubery, Tarling and Wilkinson, 1982). The policy of introducing a national minimum wage was not approved until 1986 by the Trades Union Congress, when it was realized that a system of incomplete collective bargaining associated with Wages Councils would not provide effective protection of low-paid workers.

The Wages Councils set minimum rates of pay in a limited number of low-paying sectors from 1909 to 1993. At the time of their abolition, Wages Councils operated in 26 sectors and roughly 2.5 million workers were covered, with a minority directly affected by the minima set. New rates were set each year but there were no formal indexation mechanisms. The outcome was determined by a form of surrogate collective bargaining in which independent members were final arbiters when employer and employee representatives were unable to reach agreement. The rates set were very low, and there is some evidence of non-compliance even with these low rates.

Compared to the UK, France has a tradition of seeking to regulate wages in general through widespread collective bargaining. After 1945, most branches of industry had collective agreements that extended to all employers in the sector, and set minimum rates that were legally binding. To fill the remaining gaps, a national minimum wage was introduced in 1950 but with a complicated system of sub-minimum rates that varied by region and town. Over the subsequent eighteen years, these lower rates were phased out. Furthermore, by the end of the 1960s there was increasing dissatisfaction with the way in which the minimum wage had declined relative to overall earnings (even though it did not decline in real value). In 1970, a new minimum wage was introduced with stated aim of ensuring that the lowest paid workers enjoyed the benefits of economic growth.

From 1970 onwards, the national minimum wage has been indexed in two ways. First it rises in line with retail prices. On July 1st of each year it is raised to cover the rise in retail prices since the last uprating. In between times, it is uprated every time the price index increase rises by 2%. In this way the real value of the minimum wage can never fall by more than 2% at any one time and it cannot fall at all in the twelve month period between July 1st of each year. Secondly, the minimum wage is partially indexed on real earnings, and indirectly on productivity growth. The minimum must rise in real terms on an annual basis by at least half the real increase in manual workers' earnings.

The minimum wage will thus tend to rise in real terms over time. However, the application of these indexation mechanisms alone means that the minimum wage will decline as a proportion of average earnings. Thus, in practice, increases went beyond the application of the legal indexation requirements, as successive governments implemented discretionary increases. In the twenty eight years of its existence, discretionary increases have been implemented in twenty four years. These have had the effect of increasing the minimum wage relative to average earnings at certain times. Overall, the minimum wage has been uprated on a regular basis and has remained an effective means of protection for the low paid in France during the period covered.

In the Netherlands, a statutory national minimum wage has existed since 1969. It has national coverage and is formally indexed on average earnings. The full rate is payable for workers aged 23 or over, with differential rates beginning at 30% for 15-year-olds. The minimum wage legislation underwent modifications during the 1980s. In 1984, its level was reduced in nominal terms and it remained frozen – i.e. the formal indexation mechanism was suspended – at that level for the remainder of the 1980s. In addition the differential rates for young persons were reduced on two occasions prior to 1984 in the hope that this would increase youth employment. Towards the end of the 1980s and in the early 1990s the minimum wage was uprated in line with average wages again, only to be frozen once more between July 1992 and December 1995.

Figure 2.6 shows how the minimum wage declined relative to median earnings in the Netherlands while in France it increased substantially during the first half of the 1980s and then slipped back. It finished at a higher level relative to median earnings in the 1990s compared to the late 1970s. The extent of low pay in the Netherlands appears to grow from the time the minimum wage was reduced and frozen. In France, the evolution is less closely related. The reduction in the relative value of the minimum wage after 1984 is associated with only a slight increase in low paid employment.

3   THE 1980s: DIVERGENT APPROACHES

The United Kingdom

At the end of the 1970s, unemployment was rising in a number of countries following a slow down in growth after the oil price shocks of 1973–4 and 1978–9. Many countries were finding it difficult to keep inflationary

Figure 2.6a
Minimum wages relative to median earnings (%)

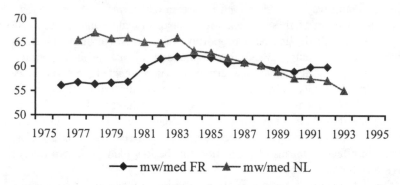

Figure 2.6b
Minimum wages relative to median earnings NL (%)

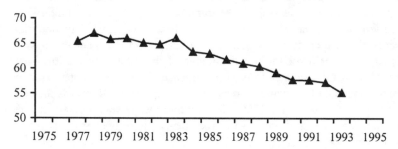

Figure 2.6c
Minimum wages relative to median earnings FR (%)

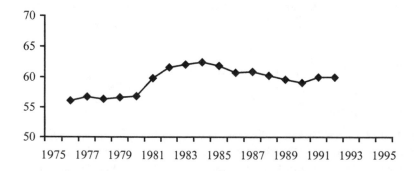

pressures under control without exacerbating the unemployment problem. The change of government in the UK in 1979 brought a new policy of reducing the power of trades unions and deregulating the labour market. As far as low-paid workers were concerned, measures such as the Fair Wages Resolution (which ensured that firms working on public sector contracts paid the wage rates set in public sector collective agreements) were abolished, so that in the case of the FWR, the contracting-out of privatized services led to lower wages for many cleaners and security staff. The Wages Councils system were threatened with abolition on two occasions – 1985 and 1988 – and reprieved because a number of employers wanted to maintain it. From 1988, young persons under the age of 21 were excluded from their scope. Over time, the relative value of Wages Councils minima has declined as a proportion of average earnings. Thus over the 1980s minimum wage protection was progressively weakened in Great Britain only to be abolished in August 1993. At the same time the coverage of collective bargaining has fallen as has union density. The balance of bargaining power has increasingly shifted towards employers as a result of these trends, higher unemployment levels and a series of changes in industrial relations legislation.

France

The opposite of this approach prevailed in France from the early 1980s. The newly elected Socialists increased the minimum wage by 10% in one fell swoop in 1981 (see Bazen and Skourias, 1997 for an analysis of this episode), reduced the length of the working week and reinforced collective bargaining arrangements with a new law. There was an attempt to expand the economy which was abandoned in 1983, and thereafter the control of inflation became a priority. This was achieved however, not through labour market deregulation but through restrictive macroeconomic policy and maintaining a strong Franc. Wage-setting adjusted to this framework to the extent that over the period 1985–96, the share of wages in national income fell by 10 percentage points.

The French economy avoided the sharp recessions experienced by the United Kingdom, and employment levels did not drop sharply. However, the rate of net job creation was insufficient to absorb the increase in the active labour force so that unemployment has steadily risen, and this led to the large-scale use of special employment measures for young persons and the long-term unemployed. The protection afforded by the minimum wage has not been modified in formal terms, but a number of these employment measures permit firms to pay less than the minimum wage (see Balsan, D.Werquin, Hanchane, S. and Werquin, P., 1998). Another consequence has been the compression of wage differentials among the low paid due to the failure of collectively agreed wage rates to keep pace with the national minimum wage.

This led in 1990 to the Socialist government calling for the renegotiation of collectively agreed wage scales to establish a differential with the minimum wage. By and large this occurred, but the discretionary increase in the national minimum wage implemented following the election of Jacques Chirac as president in 1995 eliminated this differential in the majority of collective agreements. The national minimum wage has therefore been a key influence in the low-wage labour market in France, preventing the wage distribution from falling away in the face of pressure from high unemployment rates, from increasing labour market deregulation elsewhere in Europe and from the strengthening of employer power in collective bargaining. Its place has been assured by an apparent political consensus to maintain it and its use as a political gesture by presidents and prime ministers of different political persuasions. The one time when a government attempted to interfere with it by introducing what appeared to be a lower rate for under 25s, nation-wide protests forced the measure to be dropped.

The Netherlands

The Netherlands saw employment and earnings actually fall across the board in the first half of the 1980s. Since then employment (hours worked) has grown back to its original level and, recently, it has gone above that level. In a comparative perspective, however, recent Dutch employment growth has been considerable with only a temporary standstill, not even a fall, in 1993– 94. Average (hourly) earnings slowly made a comparable comeback and present levels are not much higher than those of the late 1970s. Their increase roughly coincides with employment growth. At the same time, because of its lowering and subsequent freezes, the minimum wage has lagged behind average earnings as did adult full-time minimum-wage employment compared with total employment. One could almost say that during its existence, discretionary freezes of the minimum wage have been the rule and not the exception. The initial overall decline in earnings had the approval of the trade unions – who may have been forced by circumstances – in exchange for shorter working hours. Furthermore, in the 1990s, with the threat of a new decline in employment, unions and employers swiftly agreed upon wage restraint. Since 1984 there has been a growing gap between the lowest wage rates in collective agreements and the statutory minimum wage which has aroused intense political debate. On further scrutiny, however, the gap between the minimum wage and those rates in only the relevant agreements, i.e. for the low-paid industries, appears to be much smaller, but there is a gap. In spite of the growth of low-wage employment, unemployment among the less-skilled has remained much higher than for the rest of the labour force. In the policy debate this is often blamed on a shortage of low-paid jobs in the labour market. Since 1994, the new government has decided to tackle the problem partly by funding such jobs in the public sector (municipalities) and health care, and partly by introducing a subsidy on low wages for private enterprise. The use made of the subsidy is a great success in terms of money demanded; its effects on employment, however, remain to be established.

Current Policy Stance on Low-Wage Employment

Since the mid 1990s, there have been further developments in policy on low-wage employment. The change of government in the UK in 1997 means that a national minimum wage will be introduced in 1999. Its level and the treatment of young persons are yet to be determined. However, there are no further policies to help the low paid through encouraging more collective bargaining. On the contrary, low-wage employment is to be encouraged through providing assistance to persons accepting low paying jobs through the tax-benefit system. In France, the return of the Socialists to power in the same year means that France remains committed to an active minimum wage policy. However, low-wage employment is being encouraged through the expansion of schemes to employ unemployed young persons. In the Netherlands, one can say that the minimum wage has lost most of its significance for wage earnings. Nevertheless, it is still a bone of contention partly for different reasons. It determines a large part of public spending, particularly benefits. Also, it is still attacked for ideological reasons. The thesis is that it was originally meant to maintain a family. Now it should be adapted to a single-persons household implying a lowering by thirty per cent but without taking into account its substantial fall in real terms and relative to other earnings.

4   FUTURE RESEARCH

While the way in which low-wage employment has evolved in the three countries considered here has been examined, the analysis is limited to full-time adult workers. This group contains low-paid workers, but excludes two groups in particular: part-time and young workers. Much of the concern about the future of low-paid work involves the impact on these two groups. For part-time workers, there is the question not only of wage levels but also of employment protection and access to social security benefits. For young persons, a number of issues arise. It is important for a young person to gain access to the labour market, and then move up the earnings distribution as he or she gains experience either with their current employer or by changing employers. This poses the dilemma of whether the creation of low-paying jobs is the appropriate way in which to help young workers. There is the danger that employers use the ability to employ low-paid youngsters as a means of perpetuating low-wage jobs rather than investing in up to date technology. It is hoped that the new, harmonized micro-data sets collected for Eurostat will provide more information on these groups, and enable a clearer picture of their situation to be obtained.

REFERENCES

Atkinson, A. B. and Bazen, S. (1984), The SMIC and earnings in France and Great Britain, SSRC Programme on Taxation, Incentives and the Distribution of Income, London School of Economics, Research Note No.12.

Balsan, D., Hanchane S. and Werquin, P. (1998), Sub-Minimum-Wage Employment, Earnings Profiles and Wage Mobility in Low-Skill Youth Labour Market: Evidence from French Panel Data 1989–95, in this volume.

Bazen, S. and Skourias, N. (1997), *Is There a Negative Effect of Minimum Wages on Youth Employment in France*? European Economic Review, 41 (3-5), April 1997, p. 723-732

Centre d'Etudes sur le Revenu et les Coûts (CERC) (1991), *Les bas salaires dans les pays membres la Communauté Européenne*, La Documentation Francaise, No. 101, Paris.

Craig, C., Rubery, J., Tarling, R. and Wilkinson, F. (1982) *Industrial organisation, labour market structure and low pay*, Cambridge University Press, Cambridge.

Salverda W. (1996), Minimum Wages and the Evolution of Low-Wage Employment in Western Europe and the United States over the1980s and 1990s, paper presented at the European Association of Labour Economists conference, Chania, Greece, September. (See also chapter 3 present volume)

3. Incidence and Evolution of Low-Wage Employment in the Netherlands and the United States, 1979–1989

Wiemer Salverda

---

1   INTRODUCTION

At least five observations motivate a detailed comparison of wage inequality and low-wage employment across the Atlantic, i.e. between the United States and the Netherlands. We will start explaining these five problems and then explain how they will be tackled in this contribution. First, after 1945 Western European unemployment rates initially stayed far below American levels. Around 1980, however, the two sides swiftly traded places. Now it is often thought that European unemployment is structurally increasing, with each new recession, while American unemployment levels are much more similar to earlier decades. Behind the divergent experiences of employment are opposite differences in employment growth. Figure 3.1 shows how, after 1979, Dutch employment initially lagged behind – it actually fell – followed by a period of strong growth after which its growth went down again.

Other countries of the European Union have similar differences and their lack of employment growth has been attributed by many to what has been termed *Eurosclerosis* (e.g. Ellman 1985, Krugman 1993). The concept pictures European economies as unable to react adequately to the shocks transmitted from the world economy (cf. Theeuwes, 1995). National labour market institutions may hamper a flexible adaptation. Examples mentioned are the system of unemployment benefits, in-built lags of the consultation economy (e.g. collective agreements), and firing rules. Another example which has received particular attention is the statutory minimum wage, the institution which interferes most directly in wage formation. The popular idea is that this has obstructed the much-needed wage flexibility. Wage inequality in the Netherlands has remained more or less the same while in the United States inequality is much greater and has also increased significantly. Akin to this, low-wage employment is also much greater in the US (see Table 3.1).

25

Figure 3.1
Employment* growth in the Netherlands and the United States
Index numbers 1979=100

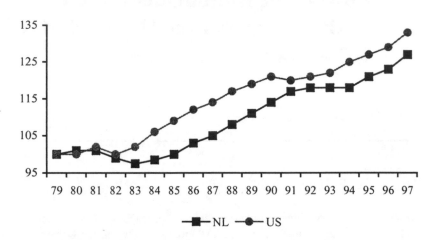

*Dependent employment 16–64 years measured in persons
Source: Bureau of Labor Statistics (BLS) and Dutch Statistics (CBS)

Figure 3.2
Average annual real growth (%) upper limit of first decile of wage
distribution, 1980–90/92

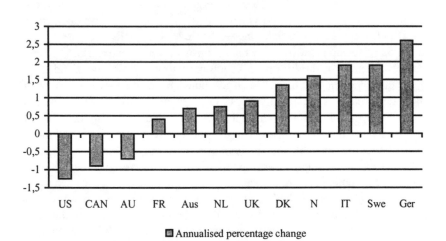

Source: OECD, Jobs Study, 1994, p. 21 and Groot, 1994

This, in turn, is related to the lower end of the wage distribution and a divergence in low-wage employment growth, as elaborated in the OECD Jobs Study (Figure 3.2). As a measure of low wages, it compared the evolution of the first decile, in real terms, contrasting an average annual increase of about 0.75 per cent in the Netherlands with a decrease of 1.3 per cent in the US.

It brings us to the second observation: present international comparisons are lacking in precision. Behind the OECD figures are significant international differences regarding earnings concepts, the populations included in the statistics or the periods covered.[1] Figure 3.1 was based on broader data on earnings distributions gathered earlier in the OECD *Employment Outlook 1993*. It is revealing that the figures mentioned in the new *1996 Outlook* are sometimes quite different. This is not a particular failure of the OECD, and fortunately in the *1996 Outlook* the OECD has become more careful in drawing conclusions from the purely macroeconomic data. It is largely a problem of statistical observation that characterizes most international comparisons as is illustrated in Table 3.2.There is much research available on US wage inequality but rather little on international comparisons

Table 3.1:

Wage inequality ratios and the incidence of low-wage employment, United States and the Netherlands, 1979–1994

	Wage inequality ratio of highest to lowest decile				Low-wage employment**
	1979	1985	1989	1994	1994 /95
United States	3.73*	3.87*	4.04*	4.35	25.0
Netherlands	2.47*	2.51	2.61	2.59	11.9

* author's estimate on the basis of same tabulated data as used by OECD
** % earning less than two-thirds of the median wage
Source: OECD, Employment Outlook 1996, chapter 3

although there are some important studies. Authors move between comparing comparable groups, e.g. only full-time employees,[2] for reasons of homogeneity on the one hand, and covering the entire economy on the other. The drawback of the former is that the approach may be much more partial in one country than in another or at one moment in time then in another; depending on the composition of employment. This limits its use for explaining differences between *national* economies especially when they

include the Netherlands, the world champion of part-time work. Paradoxically, an approach covering the entire economy can have similar drawbacks.
With the usual focus on *persons* earning a wage, differences in employment
composition, again between full-time and part-time labour, are inadequately
taken into account. For a full picture of any developed economy nowadays we
have to account for wide differences in the incidence of part-time work which
is also quickly growing in most countries. This is particularly relevant at the
lower end of the wage distribution. In the Netherlands the share of part-timers
among employees grew from about twenty per cent in 1979 to some thirty per
cent in 1995. In the US the share is at a lower level and is also more stable,
climbing only from sixteen per cent in 1979 to nineteen in 1994 (OECD,
Employment Outlook 1995, p. 210).

Table 3.2:

International comparisons of wage inequality involving the United States

Study	Wage concept, population	Differentials				
		Age	Sex	Educa-tional	Indus-trial	Regional
Davis, 1992	Weekly, full-time	X	Men			
Erikson & Ichino, 1994	Annual, full-time, full-year	X	Separate	X		
Katz *et al.*, 1995	Hourly, full-time	X	Separate	X	X	Met-ropolitan
Card *et al.*, 1996	Hourly, whites	X	Separate	X		

This brings us to a third observation. Even within one country and at one
moment in time the measures of wage inequality can differ greatly. The
international debate takes its inspiration from the American debate on
inequality which has been going on for some time. Table 3.3 shows a number
of American inequality outcomes, all of which apply the same approach based
on decile ratios, for 1979. Although all calculations are based on the same
data source (CPS) the results differ widely in level (and also in subsequent
development). Much depends on the exact earnings concept used and the
population that is captured by the survey (not shown here). It clearly implies

that one has to be very careful about all aspects in making international comparisons.

The American lead in the inequality debate has strongly influenced international comparisons, sometimes to the disadvantage of the latter – the fourth observation. In a way it is just a continuation of the American debate, now with illustrations from abroad. In the US, studies of increasing inequality are strongly focused on educational differentials and as a consequence so are many international comparisons. They relate this particular lot of wage differentials to changes in the supply and demand of labour at different training levels and usually the argument stops there. Behind the fixation is mainstream human capital theorizing. This is open to criticism.

Table 3.3:
United States wage inequality ratios, highest to lowest decile, 1979

Study	Wage concept	All	Men
Karoly, 1993, Appendix 2B2	Annual	21.50	13.79
	Weekly	8.62	7.00
	Hourly*	4.75	4.72
Mishel *et al.*, 1996, 143–4	Hourly	3.50	3.67
OECD, 1996, 62	Weekly		3.18
Davis, 1992, figure 1A	Weekly		3.37
Katz, *et al.*, 1995, 58	Hourly		3.42
Erikson & Ichino, 1994, 31	Annual		5.61

* used in OECD, Employment Outlook 1993

Given the evidence found in recent years on significant and steady inter-industry differentials, human capital variables at best are only part of the story. In an international context the restriction is even more serious. Although the rankings of industries by wage level in different countries appear to be highly correlated, the size and role of inter-industry differentials differs greatly, particularly between the US and other countries.[3] Simply shifting the focus from educational to inter-industry differentials would not be a good alternative. It is not impossible that various kinds of differentials, by age, by industry etc., are mutually compensating – how else could one explain that, if for a moment we leave aside the different employment and unemployment outcomes, the national economies usually are reasonably competitive in spite of considerably diverging educational or industry differentials. The approach chosen here for the comparison across the Atlantic is to consider the complete mix of differentials, training and industry, and see how it relates to wage inequality and low-wage employment.

Table 3.4:

Dutch minimum-wage employment, employees 16–64 years of age, 1974–1994

Number (×1000)								
	'74	'76	'79	'83a	'83b	'85	'86	'87
	372	406	365	258	226	195	183	180
	'88	'89	'90	'91	'92	'92*	'93*	'93*#	'94*#
	177	163	146	132	122	129	110	170	201
Share of employment (%)								
	'74	'76	'79	'83a	'83b	'85	'86	'87
	9.8	10.5	8.9	6.5	5.8	5.0	4.5	4.3
	'88	'89	'90	'91	'92	'92*	'93*	'93*#	'94*#
	4.2	3.8	3.3	2.9	2.7	2.7	2.3	3.2	3.7

* including sheltered workplaces
# including persons working less than one-third of the normal working week
Source: CBS, 1974–83a Minimum wage surveys; 1983b–1994 based on (Half)Yearly Earnings Surveys

Finally, a minimum wage is often seen as a handicap for a flexible adjustment of wages to changing international circumstances. This view has been an important element in the Dutch public debate for many years, and it still is. The decreasing incidence of minimum-wage employment (see Table 3.4[4]) is considered as giving evidence of the fact that the minimum wage is too high for profitably creating low-paid employment. Certainly, the strong decline of Dutch minimum-wage employment, its present rate being no more than about one-third of that of the end of the 1970s, has nourished the idea that the minimum wage is encroaching upon employment, particularly low-wage employment. We will see below that these figures can be quite misleading, but that is not the point here. The problem is the way of international comparisons of minimum wages. There is much information on the level of minimum wages but very little on their employment incidence. Often, international studies simply relate the minimum wage to employment in general without paying much attention to the distribution of employment by wage level. Consequently, there is a great need for better data, a need which we also hope to serve here.

Set-Up

In this chapter we will try to find answers to these problems by studying inequality and low-wage employment from different angles but steadily applying exactly the same type of data and concepts. Throughout we will use hourly earnings and hours worked. Hourly earnings are basically calculated as usual weekly earnings divided by usual hours worked per week. The focus is the number of hours worked (normalised as full-time equivalents, FTE, of 35 hours per week) instead of the number of persons working. It means that we cover employment in both countries in a way that is meant to neutralise the strongly diverging incidence of part-time work[5]. Hourly earnings have also been used in other research but usually in a combination with persons working instead of hours worked. Hopefully, the FTE approach will picture the labour market with more precision. Interestingly, it may also enable, in further research, a better evaluation of the significance of low-wage employment for household poverty.[6]

First, we will scrutinize the usual (macroeconomic) measures of wage inequality basing them as much as possible on identical concepts of earnings and population for the two countries. Next, we sketch the changes in low-wage employment between the two countries and over time. We will apply five different definitions. Four are taken from the literature to find out if they behave differently:

a) the first decile as used by the OECD, *b)* two-thirds of the median now also followed by the OECD after earlier EU research,[7] *c)* the real value of the first quartile of 1979 (a measure similar to the one applied by Bluestone and Harrison in their famous U-turn study), and *d)* the statutory minimum wage.

A fifth definition, the ratio of the 1979 statutory minimum wage to the median of that year, is chosen to compensate for the strong fall that has occurred in the relative level of the minimum wage in the two countries over the 1980s while at the same time avoiding the pitfalls of declining real wages.

Thirdly, and most importantly, a comparison will be made of inequalities at the micro level. A multiplicative dummy model[8] helps to describe the relative wage structure for each country/year combination:

$$W = aX + e$$

where W is the individual wage, X is the vector of characteristics and a is the coefficients that describe the structure of wages.

For the purpose of evaluating the role of state and union wage policies the wage structure is the most relevant element. It describes relative wages dependent on socio-demographic (age, sex, education) as well as job (industry, full-time/part-time) characteristics. To a certain extent it also incorporates the effects of labour market institutions that influence wages. Classifications of age and of sex match between the US and the Netherlands by definition. The educational variables, however, pose more problems. We use the highest diploma attained, also for the US, and not years of education completed which are often used. Unfortunately, diploma levels differ between the two countries. The Netherlands has a more differentiated system of secondary education, and senior secondary education plausibly attains a somewhat higher level than the American high school. Also 'first level' is after finishing elementary education and does not include 'no education' as in the US. In addition, we had to distinguish 'education unknown' for the Dutch data because an increasingly large part of the survey populations, with a concentration at the lower end of the pay distribution, would otherwise be left out. Finding a better educational match should be a matter of concern for further research although the problem might be less than it seems at first sight because the main interest here is relativities, not absolute levels. For industries we have applied the US one-digit classification but we kept wholesale trade and retail trade apart. The two are often lumped together although they show important differences in wage level and significance for low-wage employment. We mimicked the American industries as far as possible for the Netherlands except for retail trade where we followed European conventions excluding eating and drinking places. The latter are included in personal services here. Finally, for the US we added regional dummies on the assumption, first, that the country is so much larger than the Netherlands and, secondly, that there is no a priori reason to neglect their possible influence as is demonstrated by the example of steady inter-industry differentials.[9] We have not accounted for racial and ethnicity differentials in the US.

The reference group used in the dummy regression is the same in both countries: men aged 25–29, high school or senior secondary education completed, working full-time in manufacturing (and, in the US, living in the North East). The group seems to be relatively stable over time.[10] Wages are relative to the mean of this group. Their average real wages appear to behave similarly.

We will use the microlevel approach to probe into the macrolevel outcomes on inequality and find out more about the flexibility of relative wages. It helps us to distinguish, in a comparative perspective, between the effects of a changing employment composition and other factors on the evolution of inequality, and those of a changing microeconomic structure of wage levels.

Data

Finally, there are some further caveats. For the US we use CPS data which are household-based; Dutch-data, however, are employer-based. The former may be more accurate about education, the latter about earnings.[11] For the Netherlands, we could make use of three sets of microdata gathered by Dutch Statistics for 1979, 1985 and 1989. The years studied here have been dictated by this availability. Fortunately, it is a relevant set of years as it covers the rapid coming into being of the large negative Dutch employment differential and subsequent development that were presented in Figure 3.1. The fact that the cycle may differ between the years, might add to the interest of the comparison and should be accounted for in further research; generally, the international debate on inequalities takes little notice of the cyclical aspect. The numbers of observations are comparatively small, especially in 1985, and information on training levels is increasingly missing, up to twenty-seven per cent of the sample in 1989.[12] As this seems to imply a certain bias against youth, women, part-time work, industries such as retail trade and, consequently, against low pay in general[13] we included 'educational level unknown' as a separate variable. Dutch data for 1979 do not cover agriculture, and for an adequate comparison we also left out this sector in 1985 and 1989. Finally, between 1979 and 1989, the large-scale shortening of the working week by means of additional holiday entitlements (but of a different status) has changed the statistical registration of earnings and hours worked.[14]

2   LOW-WAGE EMPLOYMENT AND WAGE INEQUALITY IN THE UNITED STATES

Inequality

We tackle macrolevel inequalities first before going on to discuss the incidence of low-wage employment and microlevel inequalities and the structure of wages. We take 1979 as a starting point and subsequently describe the evolution to later years.

The FTE approach tends to be slightly more positive about real wage change than the persons approach. Between 1979 and 1989 prices increased by 71 per cent and the average real hourly wage rate fell by one per cent, as against two for the persons approach. Table 3.5 shows the decile values and the corresponding inequality ratios which result from the two approaches.

Although the FTE approach does not seem to make much difference to the outcomes in the same year, it does have an interesting effect on the evolution of inequality. Between 1979 and later years the effects go in opposite directions. Overall inequality, 9th to 1st decile, grows significantly less in FTE terms: plus twenty-four per cent instead of thirty-two. Also, what happens in both halves of the distribution looks different now. The increase in inequality in the lower half, D5:D1, is significantly smaller, fourteen per cent as against twenty-three if measured for persons. Behind this is a mitigated fall of the first decile (-15 instead of -20%) and a fall of the median (-3 instead of -1%). The development of the 9th decile is left virtually unchanged. Evidently, the FTE approach has its largest effect at the lower end which points to a concentration of part-time workers.

Table 3.5:

Inequalities in the American distribution of hourly wages, 1979/1985/1989

Deciles and inequality ratios	D9	D5	D1	D9:D1	D9:D5	D5:D1
1979						
All	$10.02	$5.08	$2.92	3.43	1.97	1.74
FTE	$10.41	$5.42	$3.00	3.47	1.92	1.81
1985						
All	$15.00	$7.50	$3.65	4.11	2.00	2.05
1979=100	150	148	122	120	102	118
real*	101	100	84			
FTE	$15.56	$7.78	$3.87	4.02	2.00	2.01
1979=100	149	144	127	116	104	111
Real	101	97	87			
1989						
All	$18.08	$8.55	$4.00	4.52	2.11	2.14
1979=100	181	168	137	132	107	123
Real	106	99	80			
FTE	$18.75	$9.00	$4.36	4.30	2.08	2.06
1979=100	180	166	145	124	108	114
Real	105	97	85			

* generally the price index of IMF, International Financial Statistics is used here
Source: author's calculations from CPS microdata

Low Pay

In Table 3.6 we take a look at the incidence of American low-wage employment according to the five definitions mentioned before. By definition, there is no change over time in the *incidence* of low pay if it is defined as the current first decile; the corresponding pay level of the decile is more interesting. It underwent a large fall in real terms: some fifteen per cent. This compares 'favourably' with the fading away of the real minimum wage which, between 1979 and 1989, fell by thirty-two per cent. The incidence of minimum-wage employment diminished much faster, particularly after 1985. It even fell in absolute terms and in 1989 there was only thirty-eight per cent left of its 1979-incidence. The fall of real earnings at the bottom end is mirrored in the twelve per cent increase of employment below the real 1979-quartile, a measure which keeps the threshold at an unchanged real earnings level. It is also mirrored in what happens below the minimum wage to median ratio of 1979. The incidence goes up very considerably between 1979 and 1985 and stabilizes afterwards. Finally, the two-thirds-of-the-median measure shows a fourteen per cent increase up to 1985. Its level does not seem to change much after 1985.[15] Summarizing, we can say that there is an increasing disparity between the definitions of low pay, a less than three-fold difference at the start develops into an almost ten-fold difference in 1989. It emphasizes the necessity of specifying precisely what definition is being used when we speak about low pay.

Table 3.6:

Incidence of low pay, FTE, United States, 1979/1985/1989

Amounts in $ and % shares in employment

	D1		2/3 * D5		Q1-1979		Minimum wage absolute		Minimum wage % median 1979	
	$	%	$	%	$	%	$	%	$	%
1979	3.00	10	3.61	22.0	3.75	25.0	2.90	7.7	2.90	7.7
1985	3.87	10	5.19	25.1	5.56	28.6	3.35	5.0	4.16	13.5
1979=100	127	-	144	114	148	114	116	64	143	174
Real	85		97		100		78		97	
1989	4.36	10	6.00	25.8	6.40	28.8	3.35	3.0	4.82	13.2
1979=100	145	-	167	117	171	115	116	39	166	170
Real	85		98		100		68		97	

Wage Structure

There is a notable change in inequality and low-wage employment at the macroeconomic level but this could equally well be the result of a change in the structure of wages at the individual level as a result of a changing composition of employment and other factors. We will now attempt to distinguish between the effects.

We have thus regressed hourly wages on a mixture of personal and job characteristics for reasons that were explained before. Table 3.A.1 presents the results in detail. The explanatory power of the regression is rather steady in spite of the great changes that occurred. The mean real wage of the reference group decreased by six per cent, which is below the total average. We find very large negative differentials in agriculture and personal services. These industries are almost forty per cent below manufacturing. Also, the importance of distinguishing between wholesale trade and retail trade is borne out by the large difference. Generally, industry differentials tend to become narrower over time. The importance of inter-industry differentials – they almost match the educational differentials – substantiates the necessity of taking them into account along with personal characteristics.

The least-skilled are in general 30–35 per cent below the reference level. The largest, and rapidly increasing, positive differential is found for college graduates: up to forty-seven per cent in 1989. Consequently, and in line with the outcomes of other research, educational differentials are continuously tending upward. The mining sector and people aged 35 or more also have positive differentials, up to about a quarter more. Teenagers are well below the reference group; initially their differential falls but is restored between 1985 and 1989. We also note considerable and increasing regional differentials – the South East is particularly worse off compared to the North East but most other regions go down as well. There is a relatively large but clearly diminishing gender wage gap. However, for many women the equally sized increase in the part-time wage gap may have neutralized this.

For each characteristic Table 3.7 presents what we have called width, i.e. the ratio between the minimum and maximum value of the coefficients within each group of dummies. These ratios, excluding regions for the sake of comparability with Dutch outcomes, are taken together by multiplication in 'all widths' at the end of the table. Its use will be discussed later.

Inequality and Low Pay Revisited

What are the implications for overall inequality? As a first step towards finding an answer we have multiplied the widths of the categories of differentials. Table 3.7 shows a thirteen per cent increase. It implies that potentially there is room for increasing inequality, but what will actually happen depends on the composition of employment. Therefore, we simulated the 1979 distribution of relative wages applying the wage structures of 1985 and 1989 respectively to 1979 employment:

$$\text{Wsim}_{t,1979} = a_t X_{1979} + e_{1979} \quad (t = 1985, 1989)$$

Thus the composition of employment was kept constant while the coefficients found for later years were projected onto the corresponding individual and job characteristics. The residuals of 1979 have been kept as they were to also sort out other effects than those of composition. The simulated outcomes allow splitting off the effects of the changing structure of relative wages from the changes in inequality that occurred between 1979 and later years.

Table 3.7:

Widths* of US relative wage coefficients, 1979/1985/1989

	1979	1985	1989	1979=100
Age	1.55	1.62	1.58	105
Gender	1.33	1.25	1.23	92
Full-time/ part-time	1.12	1.19	1.21	107
Education	1.92	2.11	2.23	117
Industry	2.01	1.97	1.86	92
All widths	8.60	10.03	9.69	113

* Max/min-ratios in categories of coefficients
see: Table 3.A.1 in the Appendix to this Chapter.

Table 3.8, panel A, presents the macrolevel inequalities of the original and simulated distributions. The mutual differences indicate the contributions of the changing structure of wages to overall inequality over the period, naturally given the situation at the outset. Changing differentials appear to have contributed relatively little to the growth in macrolevel inequality. The ratio of the highest to lowest decile increased by twenty-four per cent between 1979 and 1989, as we have seen in Table 3.5, but the wage structure appears to have contributed only six per cent. The first decile fell, but only by four per cent now, while the ninth slightly increased its value by two per cent. Consequently, the main causes for the increase have to be sought elsewhere. The changing composition of employment is an important candidate but non-observed individual effects, other than those of the characteristics studied here, could also play a role. The much debated within-group inequality and/or firm effects as mentioned by Blau and Kahn may be part of this.

Panel B of the table shows that if we apply the differentials of later years, minimum-wage employment would have been larger than it was in 1979 and even much larger than it actually was in 1985 or 1989. So the change in the US employment structure has been away from the official minimum wage and the increasingly lower level of pay associated with it. Minimum wage incidence fell by seventy per cent because of other influences.

Table 3.8:
Inequalities in the simulated United States wage distributions, FTE, 1979

A. Inequalities		D9:D1	D9:D5	D5:D1
a. Original 1979		3.47	1.92	1.81
b. Original 1985		4.02	2.00	2.01
c. Simulated 1985 onto 1979		3.65	1.94	1.88
d. Effect of differentials change	(c/a)	105	101	104
e. Other effects (b/a-c/a)		110	103	107
f. Original 1989		4.30	2.08	2.06
g. Simulated 1989 onto 1979		3.68	1.96	1.88
h. Effect of differentials change	(g/a)	106	102	104
i. Other effects (f/a-g/a)		117	106	110
B. Low-wage employment incidence		Minimum		2/3 * D5
(% of employment)		wage		
j. Original 1979		7.7 %		22.0 %
k. Original 1985		5.0 %		25.1 %
l. Simulated 1985 onto 1979		10.3 %		22.8 %
m. Effect of differentials change	(l/j)	133		104
n. Other effects (k/j-l/j)		48		110
o. Original 1989		3.0 %		23.3 %
p. Simulated 1989 onto 1979		10.5 %		23.0 %
q. Effect of differentials change	(p/j)	136		106
r. Other effects (o/j-p/j)		29		99

Source: author's calculations from CPS microdata

3.   LOW-WAGE EMPLOYMENT AND WAGE INEQUALITY IN THE NETHERLANDS

Inequality

We now turn to what happened in the Netherlands. Table 3.9 shows the macrolevel inequalities for both the unweighted and full-time equivalent employment. It makes some difference to the decile levels but the resulting ratios are amazingly the same. Evidently, discounting part-time workers as full-time equivalents appears to lift the entire distribution but in such a way that mutual ratios are kept intact. In 1979, the first decile is raised by less than two per cent, the ninth decile by somewhat more than one per cent; the difference is hardly perceptible through the D9:D1-ratio. Even if we focus on the weekly wages of only full-time employees it hardly makes a difference.

Table 3.9:
Inequality ratios in the Dutch distribution* of hourly wages, October 1979/1985/1989

Deciles and ratios	D9**	D5**	D1**	D9:D1	D9:D5	D5:D1
1979						
All	23.93	14.45	9.43	2.54	1.66	1.53
FTE	24.20	14.79	9.60	2.52	1.64	1.54
FT-ww***				2.52	1.65	1.53
1985						
All	27.80	17.08	11.65	2.39	1.63	1.47
1979=100	116	118	124	94	98	96
Real	88	90	94.0			
FTE	28.35	17.44	11.77	2.41	1.63	1.48
1979=100	117	118	123	96	99	96
Real	89	90	93			
1989						
All	29,87	18.07	11.49	2.60	1.65	1.57
1979=100	125	125	122	102	99	103
Real	93	93	91			
FTE	30.54	18.55	12.06	2.53	1.65	1.54
1979=100	126	125	126	100	101	100
Real	94	93	93			

* excluding agriculture ; ** Guilders ; *** Full-time, weekly wages; consistent with OECD, Employment Outlook 1993, 160 which only presents data for 23+
Source: calculated from CBS microdata 1979, 1985 and 1989

Between 1979 and 1989, the average (FTE-based) hourly wage increased by twenty-five per cent, not nearly enough to compensate for the increase of consumer prices (34%) and as a consequence it fell by six to seven per cent in real terms. Between 1979 and 1985 D9:D1-inequality appeared to decline by four per cent, from 2.52 to 2.41. The decline was concentrated in the lower half of the earnings distribution. All decile wage levels witnessed a considerable fall in real terms, but less at the lower end. Between 1985 and 1989, all decile levels tended to increase but the first decile stayed behind. Consequently, inequality increased a bit and returned to its level of departure.

On balance, the entire Dutch 'wage edifice' has shifted downwards in real terms. In real terms, the first decile fell by between six and seven per cent cumulatively over the 1980s and did not display the increase presented by the OECD (Figure 3.2).

Low Pay

Table 3.10 presents the incidence of low pay according to the five definitions. Again, but now for different reasons, there is little difference between three of these measures, the first decile, two-thirds of the median and the adult minimum wage. Percentage shares are between nine and twelve per cent. Within this narrow range, however, the incidence of minimum-wage employment shows a clear fall; notably, the minimum wage itself also suffered the largest decrease in purchasing power of these measures. The fall of minimum-wage employment (12.4 to 10.0) is considerably less than in Table 3.4 (8.9 to 3.8%). This is explained by the fact that Table 3.4 did not apply an identical wage measure to all persons. Instead the adult minimum wage was used for adults (23+) while for young workers only those were counted who earned their age-dependent youth minimum wage. Thus, Table 3.4 measured the extent to which legal provisions were in effect. By contrast, in Table 3.10 all youths earning more than the relevant youth minimum wage but no more than the adult minimum wage have also been considered; evidently, their labour force fills the gap between the two tables that grew from 3.5 to more than 6 per cent.[16] Had the minimum wage been kept at the 1979 percentage of the median wage, however, its employment incidence would have been the same in the actual 1985 distribution and in 1989 it would have increased to 14.1 per cent. The real value of the 1979-quartile as a measure of low pay tells quite a different story. There is a large increase between 1979 and 1985, when a third of the work force was on this type of low pay. It is an analogue of the American U-turn, which followed from a similar definition of low wages.[17] After 1985, there was a decrease but still a substantial increase over the 1980s remained.

The differences in evolution mirror the increasing (respectively decreasing) real value of the various definitions of low pay.

Wage Structure

Table 3.A.2 in the Appendix to this Chapter presents the results of a regression analysis comparable to that for the US with the important exception that no distinction is made between regions. There are no regional data available, but we also think that in comparison to the much larger US economy the Dutch economy may be viewed as a single geographically integrated labour market. Other variables were structured along the same lines as in the US regression. For age, sex, full-time or part-time work this does not pose a problem. Also, industries have largely been modelled according to the American example. An important problem, however, remains in education. Generally, educational systems are hard to compare between countries and an absolute comparison of the qualitative levels of their output is well-nigh impossible. Consequently, we simply derived an equal number of four levels from the Dutch system while conscious of the fact that in an absolute sense the range of training levels might be more compact and mutual differences smaller than in the US. Nevertheless, as the levels are kept the same over the years changing outcomes may have some significance in a comparative perspective. As was explained before, we had to add a dummy for educational level unknown.

Table 3.10:
Incidence of low pay in the Netherlands (full-time equivalents),
October 1979/1985/1989

	D1		2/3 * D5		Q1-1979		Minimum wage		Minimum wage % median 1979	
	f	%	*f*	%	*f*	%	*f*	%	*f*	%
1979	9.60	10	9.86	10.7	11.80	25.0	10.32	12.4	10.32	12.4
1985	11.77	10	11.63	8.7	15.53	34.2	11.90	10.6	12.17	12.3
1979=100	123	-	118	81	132	137	115	85	118	100
Real	93		90		100		88		90	
1989	12.06	10	12.37	11.3	15.86	30.5	12.07	10.0	12.94	14.1
1979=100	126	-	125	106	134	122	117	81	125	114
Real	93		93		100		87		93	

Source: calculated from CBS microdata

The role of characteristics in explaining the Dutch wage distribution is considerable but slightly decreasing over time giving a somewhat larger role to other factors.

The reference group used for the regressions witnessed a five per cent fall which is slightly better than the general average. Consequently, only those groups that saw their relative wage increase by more than five per cent have been able to maintain or raise their real wage income during the period. Only part-timers and the oldest age-group succeeded.

Table 3.11:

Widths of Dutch relative wage coefficients*, October 1979/1985/1989

	1979	1985	1989	1979=100
Age	1.95	2.76	2.57	131
Gender	1.10	1.15	1.16	106
Full-time/ part-time	1.19	1.06	1.06	89
Education	1.73	1.58	1.50	87
Industry	1.29	1.49	1.37	106
All widths	5.96	7.92	6.49	114

* excluding agriculture
see Table 3.A.2

We find very large age differentials that grew considerably between 1979 and 1985 and then fell a bit. Youths saw their relative wage fall considerably between 1979 and 1985. Teenagers were hit particularly hard as they went down from a relative level of .0.63 to .0.48 in 1985 (a 24 % decrease) but subsequently crept up again to 0.52 in 1989. Given the fact that the wages of the reference group itself fell in real terms, teenagers appear to have lost up to thirty per cent of their real wage in the first period. This is certainly a consequence of the very sharp government-wrought decreases of (youth) minimum wages in 1981, 1983 and 1984 which went down in real terms by more than thirty per cent. Other young persons aged between 21 and 24 also suffered but much less. The rising relative wages of adult groups contrast sharply with this. As a result, the width of the age differentials, already particularly large, grew by thirty per cent over the 1980s.

The gender wage gap grew as well, by six per cent. The part-time/full-time gap, however, fell by eleven per cent, and was particularly small in 1989.[18] This can perhaps explain the immense popularity of part-time work in the Netherlands compared with other countries. It also helps to understand why the FTE approach makes so little difference to inequality for the Netherlands. It should be noted, however, that part-time work is still highly concentrated among women and in certain sectors of the economy which themselves have negative differentials. So, the part-time differential may be small in itself, but it generally comes 'on top' of other negative wage gaps and consequently average part-time earnings are pretty low.

Dutch inter-industry differentials are relatively small, as in many European countries and in line with observations mentioned before. Between 1979 and 1985 their width grew substantially (1.29 to 1.49) but afterwards they fell halfway back. In 1979, some sixty per cent of workers were in industries with a wage in a band of less than five per cent around the manufacturing wage. The remaining forty per cent are on average at a distance of ten per cent. Also for the Netherlands it appears to make sense to distinguish between wholesale and retail trade. The latter is at the bottom of the list.

Table 3.12:
Inequalities in the simulated Dutch wage distributions, 1979

A. Inequalities		D9:D1	D9:D5	D5:D1
a. Original 1979		2.52	1.64	1.54
b. Original 1985		2.41	1.63	1.48
c. Simulated 1985 onto 1979		2.94	1.63	1.80
d. Effect of differentials change	(c/a)	117	99	117
e. Other effects (b/a-c/a)		82	100	82
f. Original 1989		2.53	1.65	1.54
g. Simulated 1989 onto 1979		2.81	1.60	1.75
h. Effect of differentials change	(g/a)	112	98	114
i. Other effects (f/a-g/a)		90	103	88
B. Low-wage employment incidence		Minimum		2/3 * D5
(% of employment)		wage		
j. Original 1979		12.4 %		10.7 %
k. Original 1985		10.6 %		8.7 %
l. Simulated 1985 onto 1979		15.8 %		14.5 %
m. Effect of differentials change	(l/j)	127		136
n. Other effects (k/j-l/j)		67		60
o. Original 1989		10.0 %		11.3 %
p. Simulated 1989 onto 1979		15.2 %		14.2 %
q. Effect of differentials change	(p/j)	123		133
r. Other effects (o/j-p/j)		66		80

Source: author's calculations from CPS microdata

Inequality and Low Pay Revisited

On balance, differentials widen in spite of the conflicting increases and decreases. All widths taken together increased by one-third up to 1985 but then fell halfway back (see Table 3.11). What these widths mean for an economy depends on the population's distribution of the characteristics and its change. Again, we simulated the 1979 distribution with the help of the coefficients of 1985 and 1989 (see Table 3.12) to detect the effect of the differentials change. It makes a significant difference. Simulated inequality increased from 2.52 to 2.94, or by seventeen per cent during the first half of the 1980s and subsequently decreased to 2.81. The lower half of the distribution fully bore the brunt of this stretching of the earnings distribution. Other effects than those of the characteristics considered here appear to have more than compensated for this and explain the decline in macrolevel inequality found in Table 3.9. After 1985, inequality in the lower half was somewhat reduced (17 to 14%) and the other effects were also somewhat mitigated. The upper half remained virtually unchanged over the entire period.

Minimum-wage employment and two-thirds-of-the-median employment, which fell in the actual distribution, tend to increase in the simulations. Given the 1979 economy the differentials change would have increased both types of low-wage employment substantially by around thirty per cent. It is the other effects that explain the fall that actually happened to minimum-wage employment. Without the increasing effect of the changing differentials it would have decreased by one-third over the 1980s.

4   A COMPARISON OF AMERICAN AND DUTCH DEVELOPMENTS

In the preceding sections we have surveyed the evolution of wage inequality and low-wage employment in the two countries, as much as possible in a comparable way. We will now compare the results in a context of significant differences in employment growth. First, we discuss the difference made by the greater precision of the FTE-approach used here. Then we compare American and Dutch wage structures and their importance for the comparison of inequalities. Finally, differences in low-wage employment, particularly minimum-wage employment, are considered.

Inequality

The employment gaps cannot easily be traced back to general wage growth. Dutch average real hourly wages initially pursued a trail that seems to conflict with the evolution of employment. After a very considerable eleven per cent fall over the first half of the 1980s (which from a labour cost point of view s-hould have been conducive to employment growth, but it fell dramatically) they subsequently rose by four per cent over a period during which Dutch employment actually grew and outperformed the US. In contrast, the initial fall of American real wages (-4%) did coincide with employment growth. This was followed by an almost equivalent increase (+3%) over the years when American employment, although lagging behind Dutch employment, continued to grow at the same speed. On balance, Dutch real wages decreased by six to seven per cent while America's stabilized. Perhaps specific aspects of wage developments such as wage inequality, are more important in relation to employment.

The new, more accurate FTE approach that we use modifies the picture of the inequality gap that was presented in Table 3.1. The table compared weekly earnings of American full-time workers aged 25 years or older with the annual earnings of Dutch full-time workers. The newly found inequality levels, which also cover women and part-time workers, are considerably different. American FTE-inequality still largely exceeds Dutch FTE-inequality and grew from 38 to 70 per cent of the Dutch level which is considerably more than in Table 3.1 (from 51 to 54%). The new increase is somewhat less than for the non-FTE-inequality gap which went up from 35 to 74 per cent.

The outcomes also underline the relevance to international comparisons of distinguishing between inequalities in the upper (D9:D5) and the lower half (D5:D1) of the earnings distribution (cf. Blau & Kahn 1996). The period split, before and after 1985, is also of some importance but primarily for Dutch inequality: an initial fall was followed by an equal increase. The increase in the inequality gap is largely concentrated in the first half of the 1980s. It seems to correspond nicely with the differences in employment performance which were to the advantage of the American economy before 1985.

Finally, the divergence of the lowest deciles, after deflation, as sketched by the OECD (Figure 3.2) is halved by the FTE-approach. The two per cent difference between the US (-1.30) and in the Netherlands (+0.75) is replaced by a one per cent gap (-1.60 versus -0.67).

Wage Structure

We regressed log hourly wages on personal and job characteristics to determine the relative wage structure for probing behind macrolevel inequalities. We used the same reference group which in both countries happens to suffer an almost equal decline in average real wage. Table 3.13 gives a concise overview of the resulting differentials. It should first be noted that the regression explains the Dutch wage distribution better than the American but the difference tends to decrease, mainly because more of the Dutch distribution is left unexplained.

All categories of differentials show important differences across the Atlantic. Age differentials are much wider in the Netherlands, in fact they are very wide indeed. All other Dutch differentials, however, are smaller than their American analogues, particularly educational and industrial differentials. Female and part-time wage differentials are also considerably larger in

America, and surprisingly move in opposite directions within and between both countries. The findings confirm the general idea that educational differentials have fallen in Europe, in sharp contrast with the US. The best educated especially have suffered a considerable decline in relative wages in the Netherlands. Their positive differential fell from 1.38 to 1.23 and the total width of the educational differentials went down by thirteen per cent. It may, however, to some extent be explained by the budgetary policy of the Dutch government. Since 1979 the salaries of civil servants and employees in subsidized sectors (mainly in professional services) have been considerably lowered. For many years their salaries were 'frozen' and in 1984 they even experienced a nominal decrease of three per cent, which is also what happened to the minimum wage and unemployment benefits. This was done with the explicit aim of furthering employment growth through lowering the taxation part of gross wages. As a consequence, the public sector's pay differential has suffered a massive decrease – from thirteen per cent above the reference level in 1979 to four below in 1989. The decrease relates to the educational differential as relatively many of the college-educated have a job in the public sector. However impressive the fall is, it is only part of the story. In the rest of the economy (excluding public administration and professional services) the college differential also fell. This broader effect may be associated with general government and union policies of wage moderation without hurting the lowest wages too much. In addition, bumping down and crowding out in the labour market may be important factors mitigating educational differentials. In a time of high unemployment people with a better education may accept jobs at a lower level of skill and pay and thus lower the average wage for higher levels of training.[19] Unfortunately, we could not correct for that.

Inequality Revisited

If we leave out the gender wage gap, which is generally considered an unacceptable sign of discrimination, and the part-time wage gap, which may. be related to it, the overall width of differentials as shown in Table 3.13 appears to increase much more in the Netherlands between 1979 and 1985 and even comes close to the US level. After 1985, however, the Dutch width goes down considerably more than in the US. On the Dutch side the width hinges crucially on the large teenage wage gap. This may be a basic weakness of the Dutch wage structure as a decline of teenage employment will impair the materialization of such potential inequalities. Still, on balance Dutch width grew more. Finally, a considerable part of the inequality gap relates to solid regional differences in the American labour market, which we assumed to be absent in the Netherlands.

The comparison of widths considers the two wage structures from the point of view of their potential effect for exactly the same economy. More important is the determination of their significance for inequality given the differences between the two economies. We therefore split the changes in inequality into the effects of the characteristics which comprise the wage structure, and remaining effects. Table 3.14, panels A and B, reproduces the results, shown earlier, of simulating the evolved wage structure of later years onto the original economy of 1979 for each country separately. In the first sub-period Dutch inequality grew much faster than American, but it declined during the second period while American inequality still increased.

Table 3.13:

Widths* of American and Dutch wage differentials, 1979/1985/1989

	US			.NL		
	1979	*1985*	*1989*	*1979*	*1985*	*1989*
R^2 (adjusted)	.410	.422	.403	.621	.621	.584
Age	1.50	1.62	1.58	1.95	2.76	2.57
Sex	1.33	1.25	1.23	1.10	1.15	1.16
Ft/pt	1.12	1.19	1.21	1.19	1.06	1.06
Education	1.92	2.11	2.23	1.73	1.58	1.50
Industry	2.01	1.97	1.86	1.29	1.49	1.37
Age × education × industry	5.79	6.73	6.56	4.37	6.51	5.28
Region	1.24	1.32	1.41			

* Maximum differential in each category divided by minimum

For each of the two halves of the distribution the picture is strikingly different. Over the 1980s, Dutch lower-half inequality is fully responsible for inequality growth as upper-half inequality fell. In the US, inequality grew in both halves albeit less in the upper half. In addition, Dutch lower-half inequality growth largely exceeded that in America. It is a particularly interesting finding as it implies that in a comparative perspective the lack of Dutch low-wage employment growth does not at all relate to relative wages, including the effects of the statutory minimum wage. Upper-half inequalities evolve in a noticeably different way: a relatively small increase in the US confronts a considerable decrease in the Netherlands. As was said before, this is partly the result of deliberate government budget cuts and general wage moderation policies.

In addition to the countrywise simulations, the results of some cross-country simulations are presented in panels C and D. First, the American structure of relative wages is projected onto the Dutch economy for each of the three years in question:

$$W_{NL,t} = a_{US,t} \, X_{NL,t} + e_{NL,t} \quad (t = 1979, 1985, 1989)$$

Agriculture was left out as it was not included in Dutch data for 1979, government and professional services have also been left out as there are some doubts about the exact comparability of the two sectors between the two countries. Dutch residuals were kept as they are. It implies that possible unmeasured effects, part of which may be related to labour market institutions, have not been copied from the US.

Table 3.14:
Simulated effects of relative wages on inequality, 1979/1985/1989 (%)

	D9:D1	D9:D5	D5:D1
A. Projecting 1985 wage differentials onto 1979 employment			
US	+5.2	+1.0	+3.9
NL	+16.7	-0.6	+16.9
B. Projecting 1989 wage differentials onto 1979 employment			
US	+6.1	+2.1	+3.9
NL	+11.5	-2.4	+13.6
C. Projecting US wage differentials onto Dutch employment of the same years			
1979	+4.4	+1.3	+3.1
1985	+17.3	+2.5	+14.4
1989	+14.2	+4.9	+9.4
D. Projecting US wage differentials of various years onto Dutch 1979 employment			
1979 coefficients	+4.4	+1.3	+3.1
1985 coefficients	+10.4	+4.5	+5.6
1989 coefficients	+9.2	+5.8	+3.1

Introducing the American structure would make a difference to the first decile, lowering it by three per cent, but would have left the median and the ninth decile more or less as they are. For the earnings distribution as a whole, this would have increased Dutch inequality in 1979 (D9:D1-ratio) by four per cent, which is surprisingly little given the much larger gap of almost forty per cent that actually existed (Tables 3.5 and 3.9). The difference was mainly located in the lower half of the distribution. This is consistent with observations like those of Blau and Kahn that the main inequality gap between the US and other countries resides in a larger American interval between the bottom and the median while upper-half inequalities are very similar. The larger inequalities that US relativities would produce for exactly the Dutch economy can also be interpreted as unnecessary, certainly in a static sense as apparently smaller Dutch inequalities did the job, and possibly also in a dynamic sense unless it could be shown that they would be essential to further employment growth.

In 1985, the adoption of US wage relativities would have lowered the first decile substantially more (-13%), kept the median unchanged and increased the ninth decile (+3%). Consequently, the effect on overall inequality would have been considerable, now some seventeen per cent more. The divergence is primarily concentrated in the lower half. The observation that upper-half inequalities tend to equate those of the US is still roughly correct. Between 1985 and 1989, there was some upward movement in the first decile and downward in the median (2%) and the ninth decile stayed in the same position. This explains that overall and lower-half inequality fell and upper-half inequality increased.

In panel D, the evolution of the American wage structure is projected onto the Dutch wage distribution of 1979:

$$W_{NL,1979} = a_{US,t} X_{NL,1979} + e_{NL,1979} \ (t = 1979, 1985, 1989)^{20}$$

Thus the composition of the economy is kept unchanged over the years in contrast with panel C. Overall inequality would still change under the leverage of US wages, mostly in 1985. On balance, the effects on lower-half inequality are unchanged and the influence of the changing US differentials is fully focused on the upper half. At the end of the 1980s, the upper-half gap is more important than the lower-half gap. It confirms the situation sketched in panels A and B. Apparently, the large effects on the lower-half gap found in panel C are primarily due to other effects such as the changing composition of the economy. The opposite holds for the upper-half inequality gap of 1989 – it results from the changing wage structure and not so much from the changing composition.

In the actual American distribution the first decile fell by fifteen per cent which is roughly double the decline in the Dutch decile (minus 6 to 7%). The differentials effects following from the in-country simulations, however, turn the picture upside down: the Dutch decile fell by ten per cent, the American by only four. It is other effects that bridge the gap, largely increasing the fall of the US first decile and mitigating its fall in the Netherlands. Importing into the Dutch wage distribution (of 1979) the *changes* in the American wage structure, which supposedly incorporate the fall of the US minimum wage, would not have benefited Dutch low pay over the 1980s. The large American decrease is mainly caused by the 'other effects', part of which, in the frame-work of international comparison, are the differences in the evolution of prices used to deflate earnings. The American price level increased at double the rate of Dutch prices: 71 against 34 per cent between 1979 and 1989.

We can conclude that the focus on the structure of relative wages fundamentally alters the view on inequality as being beneficial to employment growth. Table 3.15, panel A, shows for each of the two sub-periods separately, how employment growth in the two countries compares to the evolution of apparent macrolevel inequality and its lower and upper-half parts as presented in Tables 3.5 and 3.9. It confirms the 'easy view' that more inequality is good for employment and that less is damaging to employment growth, and the American case (1979–1985) seems to demonstrate that one needs quite a lot of the bitter medicine for it to have an effect. Also, there is no linear relationship as employment growth is at about the same level in both periods but inequality growth during the first period is double that of the second period. The 1979–1985 decrease in both inequality and employment in the Netherlands points in the same direction.

Table 3.15:
Employment growth and changes in inequality (%)

	1979–85		1985–89	
	US	NL	US	NL
Employment	+9	0	+10	+10
A. Macrolevel inequality				
Total (D9:D1)	+16	-4	+7	+5
Upper half (D9:D5)	+4	-1	+4	+1
Lower half (D5:D1)	+11	-4	+2	+4
B. Simulated inequality				
Total (D9:D1)	+5	+17	+1	-4
Upper half (D9:D5)	+1	-1	+1	-2
Lower half (D5:D1)	+4	+17	0	-3

In contrast, corrected for composition and other effects, simulated inequality (panel B) relates in a much more problematic fashion to the evolution of employment. First, the importance of other effects in the American case seems to suggest that much more is needed for employment growth than a simple change in relative wages. Secondly, for the Netherlands, employment and inequality appear to move in opposite directions in both sub-periods. The initial lack of employment growth occurs in spite of a very large increase in simulated inequality that exceeds American inequality growth by far. The rapid growth of Dutch employment during the second half of the 1980s was accompanied by a fall in inequality. The situation is especially telling for lower-half inequality. The implication is that for the Netherlands also, other effects play an essential role to explain this and the main question is how they relate to employment destruction before 1985 and employment creation afterwards. Simply copying known American differentials in the Netherlands would, over the decade, have made no difference to the lower end of the earnings distribution.

Low-Wage Employment

The important question is, what does all this mean for low-wage employment on both sides of the Atlantic. The different definitions that we consider lead to different outcomes within and between countries.

What might arguably be the most sensible measure of low pay from an economic point of view, the real value of the first quartile of the 1979 distribution, shows a larger increase in the Netherlands over the 1980s (see Table 3.16). Defined as two-thirds of the median, however, American low-wage employment was more than double the Dutch figure and tended to increase while in the Netherlands it was stable over time.

Table 3.16:

Low-wage employment, United States and Netherlands, 1979/1985/1989
Incidence as percentage of total employment

	2/3*D5		Q1-1979		Minimum wage			MW*		Mwsimulated	
	US	NL	US	NL	US	NL	NL#	US	NL	US	NL
1979	22.0	10.7	25.0	25.0	7.7	12.4	7.0	7.7	12.4	7.7	12.4
1985	25.1	8.7	28.6	34.2	5.0	10.6	5.1	13.5	12.3	10.3	15.8
1989	25.8	11.3	28.8	30.5	3.0	10.0	4.7	13.2	14.1	10.5	15.2

* Ratio minimum wage to median of 1979
# employment up to the weighted minimum wage

Finally, we turn to low-wage employment as defined by the minimum wage, the prime labour market institution influencing wages. Table 3.16 presents three different aspects: *a)* actual minimum-wage employment, including a weighted measure for the Netherlands,[21] *b)* employment up to the 1979 ratio of the minimum wage to the median (MW*), and *c)* minimum-wage employment as found in the in-country simulations (Mw simulated).

Figure 3.3:

Real minimum wage, US and the Netherlands, 1979–1996
Index numbers 1979=100; deflated by national consumer prices (IMF series)

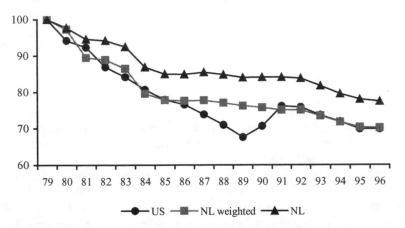

In all years, the share of plain minimum-wage employment was significantly higher in the Netherlands than in the US. It went down in both countries, but much more in America. There its incidence fell by 62 per cent and in the Netherlands by 29 per cent. This seems to correspond with the (major) fall of the real minimum wage in the two countries (see Figure 3.3): 32 and 16 per cent respectively. The Dutch weighted minimum wage, however, fell almost in line with the US minimum wage but its employment share fell less. In the Netherlands, it is often deplored that the lowering of the minimum wage has not provoked a rapid growth of low-wage employment but has gone hand in hand with a decrease of minimum-wage employment instead. It is not widely known that the same thing has happened on an even larger scale in the US.

The fall in the real value of the minimum wage substantially reduced its position in the earnings distributions. In the US it fell from 54 to 37 per cent of the median wage, in the Netherlands from 70 to 64 per cent (the weighted minimum fell from 59 to 50 per cent). The erosion of the minimum wage is aptly illustrated by the incidence the 1979 minimum wage would have had according to the 1985 or 1989 in-country simulations. It would have grown in equal measure, from a level of eight to ten per cent in the US, and from twelve to fifteen per cent in the Netherlands. After 1985, the quick further erosion of the American minimum wage is not mirrored in its employment incidence.

MW* employment incidence showed a much faster growth in the US than in the Netherlands. This, again, illustrates the importance of the other effects.

Apparently, other effects reduced US minimum-wage employment by 75 per cent and Dutch by 40. Importing the US wage structure, from the cross-country simulations, into the Dutch economy of 1979 would have doubled minimum wage incidence – a quarter of the labour force would have earned no more than the 1979 Dutch minimum wage. It illustrates the concentration of the comparative inequality gap at the bottom of the distribution.

Table 3.17:

Spread* of average relative low-wage employment incidence for categories of characteristics, United States and Netherlands, 1979/1985/1989

	US		NL	
	Spread within categories	Spread between low pay definitions	Spread within categories	Spread between low-pay definitions
Age	6	2	37	31
Sex	2	2	4	2
ft/pt	4	2	2	2
Education	8	2	10	13
Industry	10	6	9	5

* see text

Although matters of composition are generally left out in this analysis we venture some observations on low-wage employment. In the US it is a phenomenon that is much more evenly spread among the population than in the Netherlands (see Table 3.17). For each characteristic the incidence relative to that of the entire labour force was calculated and averaged for all four definitions of low-wage employment in each of the three years. For each category of characteristics the max/min-ratio of these averages was determined, mentioned in the table as 'spread within categories'. Also, for each category, the maximum spread in any of the definition-year combinations was related to the minimum to determine the differences between the definitions - mentioned as 'spread between definitions'. In the Netherlands low-wage employment is heavily concentrated among specific age-groups, especially young workers, and to a lesser extent those with low education levels, compared to the US. In addition, the large difference for youth between definitions tells us that they are largely concentrated in the lowest pay ranges – the higher the definition of low pay the less they play a role. The same holds to a lesser extent for low levels of training. For the

remaining categories the situation is quite comparable between the two
countries. This also holds for industries notwithstanding the considerable
difference in the industrial structure of the countries and the larger negative
differentials for low-paying industries. Also, the differences between
definitions in the US are smaller in spite of the much larger divergence in
incidence and earnings levels between these definitions. This is consistent
with the more even spread between characteristics.

5   CONCLUSIONS

The simple comparison of macrolevel inequalities appears to be a weak basis
for determining policies for employment growth. Close scrutiny of the wide
and increasing Dutch–American inequality gap of the early 1980s reveals that
it is only to a limited extent related to a divergence in the structure of relative
wages. Paradoxically, when Dutch relative wages became more unequal, at a
speed that exceeded American changes, employment fell; when they subsequently became more equal, Dutch employment growth at least equalled
American growth. There is good reason to doubt if applying the American
wage model in the Dutch context would in itself be very helpful for furthering
employment growth.

Table 3.18:
Hourly wage inequality for all workers, Netherlands and United States,
1989–1992

Decile ratios	D9:D1		D9:D5		D5:D1	
	NL*	US	NL	US	NL	US
1989	2.53	5.56	1.65	2.22	1.52	2.50
1992	2.67	5.40	1.67	2.25	1.59	2.40

* The Dutch data for the two years are not necessarily entirely comparable.

Sources: Netherlands: 1989, calculated from CBS microdata for all workers (persons)
including education unknown; 1992, calculated from CBS, Data on labour and wages
of employees 1993 (table 6.3A); United States: 1989, Karoly (1993), table 2B.2; 1992,
data kindly provided by Lynn Karoly.

More research is needed to see how recent developments in the 1990s
compare to the preceding decade. On the basis of other, tabulated data (see
Table 3.18) we may expect a new interesting phase of unchanged American

and increasing Dutch macrolevel inequality. Results of the current European Structure of Earnings Survey (1995) will hopefully enable an update of the FTE-approach to inequality and the role of the wage structure, and also enable other European countries to be included on a comparable basis. Thus we can determine the extent to which the Netherlands may be viewed as *pars pro toto* for Western Europe.

Evidently, other factors than the wage structure play a very important role and further research should focus on these. As far as one of these composition effects plays a role the purported causality from inequality to employment would be reversed. This would put the focus on other factors determining employment such as labour supply (e.g. the rapid fall of Dutch youth employment will have influenced the inequality outcome given the very large youth differentials) and product demand. In particular, cross-Atlantic differences in consumer demand may be very important for low-wage employment because of its concentration in retail trade, eating and drinking places, and other sectors that depend on consumption.

APPENDIX 3.A: DETAILED OUTCOMES AND DATA

Table 3.A.1:
US regressions, 1979/1985/1989

	1979			1985			1989		
N	138413			1483504			147371		
Mean	1.836			2.189			2.328		
Std error	0.402			0.418			0.455		
R2 adj.	0.410			0.422			0.403		
F- statistic	3320			3734			3431		
	LN	s.e.	$	LN	s.e.	$	LN	s.e.	$
Constant	1.849	.004	6.27	2.179	.004	8.93	2.331	.005	10.60
Age			%			%			%
16–20	-0.234	.005	0.78	-0.278	.005	0.75	-0.256	.006	0.77
21–24	-0.113	.004	0.89	-0.160	.004	0.85	-0.151	.005	0.86
25–29			1.00			1.00			1.00
30–34	0.103	.004	1.11	0.095	.004	1.10	0.104	.004	1.11
35–49	0.164	.003	1.18	0.180	.003	1.20	0.193	.004	1.21
50–64	0.164	.004	1.18	0.193	.004	1.21	0.201	.004	1.22
Gender									
M			1.00			1.00			1.00
F	-0.284	.002	0.75	-0.225	.002	0.80	-0.206	.002	0.81
Full-time/part-time									
Ft			1.00			1.00			1.00
Pt	-0.112	.004	0.89	-0.174	.004	0.84	-0.184	.003	0.83
Education									
Elem no/nf	-0.376	.006	0.69	-0.430	.007	0.65	-0.422	.008	0.66
High nf	-0.168	.003	0.85	-0.211	.003	0.81	-0.215	.004	0.81
Coll nf			1.00			1.00			1.00
Coll+	0.275	.003	1.32	0.317	.003	1.37	0.382	.003	1.47
Industry									
Agri	-0.476	.008	0.62	-0.478	.009	0.62	-0.427	.009	0.65
Min	0.222	.010	1.25	0.202	.010	1.22	0.193	.014	1.21
Con	0.090	.005	1.09	0.039	.005	1.04	0.072	.006	1.07
Manuf			1.00			1.00			1.00
Trans	0.105	.005	1.11	0.105	.004	1.11	0.098	.005	1.10
Wholes	-0.047	.006	0.95	-0.074	.006	0.93	-0.062	.006	0.94
Retail	-0.211	.004	0.81	-0.241	.004	0.79	-0.234	.005	0.79
FIRE	-0.052	.005	0.95	-0.032	.005	0.97	0.018	.005	1.02
Bus/rep	-0.158	.006	0.85	-0.142	.006	0.87	-0.107	.006	0.90
Person	-0.384	.005	0.68	-0.407	.005	0.67	-0.368	.005	0.69
Entert	-0.204	.012	0.82	-0.226	.011	0.80	-0.209	.012	0.81
Prof	-0.156	.004	0.86	-0.148	.004	0.86	-0.113	.004	0.89
Public	0.014	.005	1.01	0.011	.005	1.01	0.046	.006	1.05
Regions									
NE			1.00			1.00			1.00
Lakes	0.056	.003	1.06	-0.016	.004	0.98	-0.088	.004	0.92
Npl	-0.022	.005	0.98	-0.070	.005	0.93	-0.172	.005	0.84
MA	-0.068	.004	0.93	-0.090	.004	0.91	-0.134	.004	0.87
SE	-0.102	.005	0.90	-0.173	.005	0.84	-0.253	.006	0.78

Table 3.A.1 (continued)

Spl	-0.059	.004	0.94	-0.047	.004	0.95	-0.187	.005	0.83
Mnt	0.009	.006	1.01	-0.011	.005	0.99	-0.129	.006	0.88
Pac	0.114	.004	1.12	0.103	.004	1.11	0.030	.004	1.03

Table 3.A.2:

Dutch regressions, 1979/1985/1989

	1979			1985			1989		
N	29271			7593			28062		
Mean	2.691			2.897			2.952		
Std error	0.237			0.240			0.259		
R2 adj.	0.621			0.621			0.584		
F-stat	2179			679			1795		
	LN	s.e.	f	LN	s.e.	f	LN	s.c.	☐
Constant	2731	.005	15.35	2.896	.009	18.10	2.954	.005	19.18
Age			%			%			%
16–20	-0.464	.006	0.63	-0.727	.015	0.48	-0.653	.008	0.52
21–24	-0.144	.005	0.87	-0.205	.009	0.81	-0.175	.006	0.84
25–29			1.00			1.00			1.00
30–34	0.120	.005	1.13	0.112	.009	1.12	0.119	.005	1.13
35–49	0.192	.004	1.21	0.229	.009	1.26	0.245	.005	1.28
50–64	0.206	.005	1.23	0.290	.009	1.34	0.289	.006	1.34
Gender									
M			1.00			1.00			1.00
F	-0.089	.004	0.91	-0.142	.007	0.87	-0.146	.004	0.86
Full–time/part–time									
Ft			1.00			1.00			1.00
Pt	-0.175	.005	0.84	-0.055	.009	0.95	-0.061	.005	0.94
Education									
Unknown	-0.070	.005	0.93	-0.068	.008	0.93	-0.039	.007	0.96
Primary	-0.231	.005	0.79	-0.237	.009	0.79	-0.204	.004	0.82
Jun second	-0.161	.004	0.85	-0.122	.007	0.89	-0.110	.004	0.90
Sen second			1.00			1.00			1.00
Coll +	0.320	.006	1.38	0.218	.009	1.24	0.204	.005	1.23
Industry									
Min	0.156	.003	1.17	0.257	.047	1.29	0.147	.031	1.16
Con	0.080	.005	1.08	-0.044	.010	0.96	-0.044	.007	0.96
Manuf			1.00			1.00			1.00
Trans	0.136	.006	1.15	-0.025	.010	0.98	0.019	.006	1.02
Wholes	0.013	.006	1.01	0.015	.011	1.02	-0.005	.007	1.00
Retail	-0.074	.006	0.93	-0.124	.011	0.88	-0.166	.007	0.85
Fire	0.040	.007	1.04	0.094	.012	1.10	0.015	.008	1.02
Bus/rep	0.007	.006	1.01	0.010	.011	1.01	-0.021	.006	0.98
Person	-0.097	.009	0.91	-0.144	.015	0.87	-0.142	.009	0.87
Entert	0.014	.013	1.01	-0.020	.020	0.98	-0.051	.015	0.95
Prof	0.097	.005	1.10	-0.017	.009	0.98	-0.040	.005	0.96
Public	0.125	.005	1.13	0.024	.010	1.02	-0.037	.006	0.96

DATA SOURCES

Netherlands

CBS (Dutch Statistics) microdata are based on (half-)yearly employer-based earnings surveys including educational characteristics provided in supplementary surveys for 1979, 1985 and 1989. The number of observations is relatively small, especially in 1985, and often training information is missing (27% in 1989). Therefore, we added a dummy 'education unknown' and estimated the missing educational levels for the simulations. Applying FTE implies a small decrease in the volume of employment. Those covered are 16–64 years of age and education is defined as the level of diploma attained.

The most important deviations from the (then) usual Dutch classification of industries are that business services include repairs, and transportation includes public utilities.

United States

CPS, Outgoing rotation groups combined into annual files.

Unedited usual weekly earnings and usual weekly hours are combined to determine hourly wages and full-time equivalents (35 hours per week).

Earnings include tips and overtime; usual weekly hours exclude holidays etc.; no correction is made for topcoding or very low wages but zero wages have been left out. For regions applied see Table 3.A.3.

Those covered are 16–64 years of age and education is defined by level of diploma attained, estimated on the basis of years of schooling completed; elementary not finished includes 'no education' (about 0.2%; $\neq$ education unknown). Retailing excludes eating and drinking places which are part of personal services here.

For US data, calculations applying FTE instead of the number of persons imply a nine per cent increase in employment volume.

Table 3.A.3:
The composition of United States regions

NE: North East

Maine, New Hampshire, Vermont, Massachusetts, Rhode Island, Connecticut, New York, New Jersey, Pennsylvania

Lakes: Lake States

Ohio, Indiana, Illinois, Michigan, Wisconsin

Npl: Norther Plains

Minnesota, Iowa, Missouri, North Dakota, South Dakota, Nebraska, Kansas

Table 3.A.3 (continued)

MA: Mid Atlantic
Delaware, Maryland, Washington DC, Virginia, West Virginia, North Caorline, South
Carolina
SE: South East
Georgia, Florida, Kentucky, Tennessee, Alabama, Mississippi
Spl: Southern Plains
Arkansas, Louisiana, Oklahoma, Texas
Mnt: Mountain
Montana, Idaho, Wyoming, Colorado, New Mexico, Arizona, Utah, Nevada
Pc: Pacific
Washington, Oregon, California, Alaska, Hawaii

Table 3.A.4:
Industries in the Netherlands and the United States

Netherlands (SBI codes)		United States
0	1 agri	Agriculture...
1	2 min	Mining
5	3 con	Construction
2, 3	4 manuf	Manufacturing
4, 7	5 trans	Transportation
61 t/m 64	6 wholes	Wholesale trade
65, 66	7 retail	Retail trade excluding Eating & drinking places
81,82, 83	8 fire	Finance & insurance
68, 84, 85	9 bus/rep	Business Services + Repair
67, 98	10 person	Personal Services including Eating & Drinking Places
95, 96	11 entert	Entertainment + Recreation Services
91, 92, 93, 94, 95	12 prof	Professional and Related Services
86, 90, 97	13 public	Public Administration

NOTES

1. More about this in Salverda, 1996.
2. E.g. Blau & Kahn, 1996.
3. Cf. Hartog *et al*, 1995.

4. The 1994 increase is to a large extent caused by an increase of jobs via temp agencies (22% are paid the minimum wage).
5. Blau & Kahn also state that it is essential to adjust for 'time input' in international comparisons. They attempt to construct hourly earnings in an indirect way on the basis of macroeconomic indicators.
6. E.g. the much cited American teenagers who earn the minimum wage but belong to high-income families – they might often have only a part-time job.
7. CERC, 1991.
8. Inspired by research from Dutch Statistics: Takkenberg & Walschots (1992) who covered 1985 and 1989.
9. Bertola and Ichino, 1995, stress the importance of such regional differences.
10. Elliott *et al.*, 1996, and Lefranc, 1996, apply (very young) reference groups that, at least in the Dutch situation underwent rapid changes in their position.
11. American wages have many peak values at simple round figures.
12. Takkenberg and Walschots (1992), who are based at the CBS, endeavoured a correction which however is absent from the data put at our disposal.
13. To illustrate, average wage growth, 1979 to 1989, is 23.8 per cent for all persons in the sample, 26.9 for those with a known education; for full-time equivalents it is 25.1 and 27.6 respectively.
14. The effects of the change could be studied for 1985. They led to a two per cent decrease of the D5/D1-ratio, a one per cent increase of upper half inequality, and subsequently a one per cent decrease of overall inequality.
15. See also Table 3.1. Although the latter is for full-time workers only, the fact is a stimulus for continuing research for later years.
16. It is an underestimation because in Table 3.10 full-time equivalents are counted, which has a downward effect compared to the figures of Table 3.4.
17. Cf. Bluestone & Harrison, 1988. A further discussion is in Salverda, 1995, for full-time employees.
18. Note the gross nature of wages – with such a small differential net part-time hourly wages may even exceed full-time wages
19. Salverda, 1997, shows the large extent of such bumping down in the present Dutch labour market. Its effects on wage inequality will be the subject of further research.
20. The same dummies were left out as in panel C.
21. It accounts for the elaborate system of youth minimum wages by weighting minimum wages with the age distribution of minimum-wage employment in 1979. Given the large share of youth in minimum-wage employment this measure is more appropriate for a comparison with a single-minimum wage country.

REFERENCES

Bertola and Ichino (1995), *Wage unequality and unemployment: United States versus Europe*, CEPR, London, Discussion Paper 1186

Blau, F. and Kahn, L. (1996), International differences in male wage inequality: institutions versus market forces, *Journal of Political Economy*, **104**, 791–837.

Bluestone, B. and Harrison, B. (1988), The growth of low-wage employment: 1963–86, *American economic review*, **78**, 124–8.

Card, D., Kramarz, F. and Lemieux, T. (1966), *Changes in the relative structure of wages and employment: a comparison*, NBER Cambridge MA, Working

Paper 5487.

CERC, 1991, *Les bas salaires dans les pays de la communauté économique Européenne*, La Documentation Française no 101, Paris.

Danziger, S. and Gottschalk, P. (1993), *Uneven tides, rising inequality in America*, New York.

Davis, S.J. (1992), *Cross-country patterns of change in relative wages*, NBER, Cambridge MA, Working Paper 4085.

Elliott R., Bell, D. and Skalli, A. (1996), The wage structure in Britain and France: an analysis of wage dispersion and the returns to human capital in the private sector of the two economies, in DARES/INSEE, *Comparaisons internationales des salaires. Actes du colloque des 1er et 2 février*, Paris, 182–197.

Ellman, M. (1985), *Eurosclerosis?*, Faculty of Economics, University of Amsterdam, Research Memorandum No. 8506.

Erikson, C. and Ichino, A. (1994), Wage differentials in Italy : market forces, institutions, and inflation, NBER, Cambridge MA, Working Paper 4922.

Groot, J. (1994), Kosten van de overlegeconomie (Costs of a corporative economy), *Economisch-Statistische Berichten*, 756–759.

Hartog, J., van Opstal, R. and Teulings, C. (1995); *Inter-industry differentials and tenure effects in the Netherlands and the US*, Discussion Paper 95-147, Tinbergen Institute, Amsterdam/Rotterdam.

Huijgen, F. *et al.* (eds) (1997), *Naar volwaardige werkgelegenheid?* (Toward fulfilling employment?), Siswo, Amsterdam.

Karoly, L.A. (1993), The trend in inequality among families, individuals, and workers in the United States: a twenty-five year perspective, in: Danziger & Gottschalk (eds), 19–97.

Katz, L.F., Loveman, G.W. and Blanchflower, D.G. (1995), A comparison of changes in the structure of wages in four OECD countries, in: Freeman, R.B. and Katz, L.F.(eds), *Differences and changes in wage structures*, University of Chicago Press, 25–66.

Krugman, P. (1993), *Inequality and the political economy of eurosclerosis*, Discussion paper 867, CEPR, London

Lefranc, A. (1996) Evolutions des distributions salariales en France et aux Etats-Unis: quelques éléments comparatifs, in: DARES/INSEE, *Comparaisons internationales des salaires. Actes du colloque des 1er et 2 février*, Paris, 141–167.

Mishel, L., Bernstein, J. and Schmitt, J. (1996), *The State of Working America 1996–97*, Economic Policy Institute, Washington DC.

OECD (1993), *Employment Outlook 1993*, Paris.

OECD (1994), *Jobs study, evidence and explanations: Part 1 Labour market trends and underlying forces of change*, Paris.

OECD (1995), *Employment Outlook 1995*, Paris.

OECD (1996), *Employment Outlook 1996*, Paris.

Salverda, W. (1995), Low pay in the Dutch economy 1972–1990, in G. Benhayoun and S. Bazen (eds), *Salaire minimum et bas salaires*, L'Harmattan, Paris, 1995, 117–148.

Salverda, W. (1996), Minimum wages and the evolution of low-wage employment and wage inequality in Western Europe and the United States over the 1980s and 1990s, paper to EALE-Conference, Crete 19–22 September.

Salverda, W. (1997), Verdringing en arbeidsmarktbeleid voor de onderkant, in J. Hartog and J. Theeuwes (eds), *Creëren van werk aan de onderkant*, Wetenschappelijke Publicaties Nationaal Vakbondsmuseum, Welboom/-Delwel, Den Haag, 55–74.

Takkenberg, D. and Walschots, J. (1992), Lonen van werknemers met verschillende opleiding (Earnings of employees by education), *Sociaal-economische maandstatistiek*, supplement no 5, 5–17.

Theeuwes, J. (1995), Internationale concurrentie en nationale instituties (International competition and national institutions), in F. Huijgen *et al.* (eds).

4.   Low-Paid Work and Poverty: A Cross-Country Perspective

Ive Marx and Gerre Verbist

1   INTRODUCTION

This contribution seeks to shed some light on the link between low pay and poverty. We present results from a 14-country comparative analysis on the basis of the Luxembourg Income Study datasets. The backdrop is the current debate about the potential social costs and benefits of an expansion of low-wage employment as an antidote for Europe's labour market problems. It is often claimed, and indeed widely believed, that even a period of sustained economic growth will not suffice to eradicate Europe's persistent long-term unemployment problem. High minimum wages and corporatist wage setting practices are routinely blamed for preventing those with few marketable skills and little work experience from gaining access to a job. Generous benefits are said to discourage the unemployed with low earnings capacity from looking for work. A familiar argument in favour of more wage flexibility is that job-seekers with few marketable skills need, first and foremost, work experience. It is often claimed that low-paid jobs provide the unemployed with a stepping-stone into work, and onto the ladder of economic mobility. Proponents of tighter benefits tend to acknowledge that many of Europe's unemployed would gain little in the short run from trading in their benefit for a low-paid job. The claim is, however, that the vast majority would see their longer-term income prospects brighten by more than a shade of grey.

Benefit reductions may well force the unemployed to look harder for work and to accept low-paid jobs, but this strategy also risks increasing financial hardship among those who see their benefit taken away or reduced, but fail to secure even a low-paid job. Even countries with highly flexible labour markets, like the United States or the United Kingdom, remain confronted with substantial unemployment among their least skilled job-seekers. In addition, the claim that low-wage jobs offer a stepping stone to better paid jobs appears to have been weakened by recent longitudinal research which suggests that mobility out of low-wage employment is limited, especially in countries where low-paid work is most widespread, and that many low-wage workers alternate between unemployment, non-employment and low-wage employment (OECD, 1997).

Another argument for removing at least some of the institutional barriers to low-wage work in Europe starts from the observation that many of Europe's unemployed are effectively seeking to acquire a second household income. Unemployment in Continental Europe is to a large extent concentrated among women, particularly less educated women. This is sometimes attributed to the fact that labour market regulations and wage setting practices in Continental Europe are still rather heavily oriented on protecting household living standards via the male breadwinner, e.g. through comparatively high minimum wages or restrictions on temporary contracts. It is sometimes suggested that unemployment rates, and, more broadly, non-employment rates for less educated women are bound to remain high in Continental Europe unless more flexible, relatively low-paid jobs are allowed to emerge in the domestic services sector. Such low-paid jobs could, moreover, well provide the many single earner households in Europe with a welcome addition to the household income package. A possible hazard, from a poverty perspective, is that enhanced wage flexibility, even if it would boost double earnership substantially, could still have an adverse impact on the living standards of households which have to make ends meet on a single wage, particularly single person and single parent households.

The aim of this explorative chapter is simply to present a number of facts that might be relevant to this debate about the potential social merits and pit-falls of an expansion of low-wage employment. Using the Luxembourg Income Study datasets, we seek to shed some light on the link between labour market performance and poverty, particularly the link between low-wage employment and poverty. We begin this chapter with a note on poverty measurement. By way of setting the stage, we explore the cross-country relationship between labour market performance and poverty. Next, we focus specifically on the relationship between low pay, the household income package and poverty. We also take a preliminary look at the impact of taxes and benefits on the financial position of low-paid workers. In a final section we draw together the evidence and we formulate a number of tentative policy conclusions.

2   ON POVERTY MEASUREMENT

Poverty in advanced societies refers to an inability to function normally in society, due to a lack of material resources. In keeping with common practice in cross-national comparative poverty research, we use a relative poverty threshold, which is fairly straightforward to calculate and to interpret.

A household is said to be in poverty if the total disposable household income, adjusted for family size (what we refer to as equivalent income), is less than 50 per cent of average equivalent income.

We measure poverty on the basis of disposable household income, which does not include non-cash transfers. Poverty is, therefore, assumed to be a household phenomenon. There is evidence of unequal divisions of income within households (Jenkins, 1991), but since this is difficult to measure we have little option but to assume that income is equally shared among household members. The equivalence factors which we use to calculate equivalent income are as follows: 1.0 for the first adult, 0.5 for each additional adult and 0.3 for every child. This equivalence scale has been widely used, and is similar to other popular choices, e.g. the square root of family size. For a further discussion of these issues we refer to Atkinson (1995), Atkinson *et al.* (1995), Callan and Nolan (1991) and Van den Bosch *et al.* (1993).

Let us add, briefly, that different measurement procedures do produce significant cross-country differences, but that similar clusters of high-poverty and low-poverty countries tend to emerge regardless of the choice of equivalence scale or poverty line. The poverty figures in this paper refer to the late 1980s and early 1990s, because more recent datasets are not available for most countries. Table 4.A.1 in the Appendix to this Chapter lists the datasets. It is perhaps useful to add that poverty rates do not tend to fluctuate wildly from one year to another. A poverty rate for one particular year in the late 1980s or 1990s can be assumed to be representative for the situation

A snapshot picture as the one we present here may well obscure a higher degree of economic mobility in high-poverty countries like the United States, Canada or the United Kingdom. Longitudinal research has revealed that there is extensive movement into and out of relative poverty but that those who escape poverty do not generally make large gains. An eight-country comparative study (Canada, France, Germany, Ireland, Luxembourg, the Netherlands, Sweden and the United States) by Duncan *et al.* (1995) suggests that a rapid escape (after one year) seems to be more likely in countries with low poverty rates (like the Netherlands and Sweden) than in countries with high poverty rates (like Canada and the United States). In other words, there appears to exist a marked *inverse* relationship between the incidence of poverty and escape rates. To some extent, this is due to the fact that the poverty threshold typically cuts higher up the income distribution in high poverty countries. Hence, the higher the income increase required to escape poverty.

A different approach, which examines escape from the bottom decile reveals essentially similar patterns of economic mobility across countries. It appears, at any rate, that high poverty countries do not enjoy significantly higher levels of economic mobility.

3   LABOUR MARKET PERFORMANCE AND POVERTY IN A CROSS-NATIONAL PERSPECTIVE

Employment Performance and Poverty

Figure 4.1, which plots poverty rates against employment rates for the early 1990s, serves to give a sense of the extent of cross-national variation in employment and poverty outcomes (see also Table 4.1). One does not expect to find a simple cross-country correlation between a country's employment and poverty rate. Countries may have comparatively high or low poverty rates

Figure 4.1

Employment performance and poverty

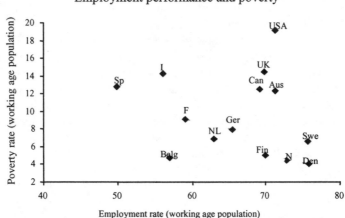

Employment rate (working age population)

for reasons which have little or nothing to do with employment performance. And yet, it is striking that the relative poverty rate for the working age population[1] in the United States is almost twice as high as in Germany or France, and almost four times as high as in Belgium, although a far higher proportion of the working age population has at least one job in the United States. Likewise, poverty at working age appears to be relatively widespread in Australia, Canada and the United Kingdom, all of which are countries with better employment records than most of the Continental European countries. That there is no inevitable 'trade-off' between work and poverty – a popular notion in Continental Europe – seems to be demonstrated by the Nordic countries, which manage to combine employment rates that are among the highest in the OECD area with poverty rates that are among the lowest. However, our graph contains data for the early 1990s. In the meantime,

Finland and to a lesser extent Sweden have seen their employment rates drop rather dramatically. Denmark and Norway, by contrast, have more or less sustained their comparatively high employment rates.

Table 4.1:
Poverty rates for the working age population in selected OECD countries

	All	By sex			By age	
		Men	Women	-25	25–54	+55
Australia	12.5	9.8	15.0	14.8	9.9	20.9
Belgium	4.7	4.1	5.2	6.3	3.2	8.1
Canada	12.3	10.8	13.7	17.2	10.3	14.9
Denmark	4.0	3.9	4.2	11.5	2.3	1.2
Finland	5.0	4.6	5.3	11.9	2.6	5.7
France	9.1	8.1	9.9	14.5	6.8	10.7
Germany	7.9	6.7	9.1	11.7	7.1	8.4
Italy	14.3	13.7	14.9	17.8	12.8	14.9
Netherlands	6.9	5.5	8.3	14.6	5.2	5.5
Norway	4.4	3.9	5.0	8.8	3.3	2.5
Spain	12.8	11.4	13.9	13.6	11.2	16.3
Sweden	6.6	6.7	6.6	25.5	2.1	1.3
UK	14.5	13.0	15.8	16.4	13.1	17.1
United States	19.1	16.8	21.2	27.4	16.8	18.2

Single Earnership and Poverty

Let us now look at the link between labour market performance and poverty at the household level, which is, after all, the most appropriate level of analysis. The living standard of a typical household at working age increasingly depends on the *combined* labour market positions of household members rather than, as was typically the case two or three decades ago, on the labour market position of the male breadwinner. Double earnership – both partners earning a wage – appears to be an almost watertight guarantee against poverty in most countries.[2] The United States is just about the only advanced economy where a very significant proportion – almost 8 per cent – of double earner couples live in poverty (Table 4.2). The United States also appears to be one of the few countries where double earner households make up a substantial proportion of all working age households in poverty (Table

4.3). In most other countries, however, it does not appear to matter much whether one or both partners has low earnings; the vast majority of two adult households with at least two earned incomes are not in poverty.

Table 4.2:
Poverty rates for various household types, working age population

	All	Single adult		Two adult household		
		In work	Not in work	Double earner	Single earner	No earner
Australia	14.5	10.1	65.6	1.1	9.0	47.5
Belgium	5.0	1.3	16.1	0.1	2.4	18.0
Canada	15.4	16.2	63.7	3.1	13.0	46.5
Denmark	6.1	8.6	20.1	0.4	2.0	7.9
Finland	7.5	12.1	30.3	1.0	1.8	8.9
France	8.4	3.8	32.5	0.2	7.8	25.6
Germany	10.4	10.5	44.2	1.5	7.0	32.4
Italy	13.3	3.2	27.1	1.2	16.3	23.5
Netherlands	8.3	12.1	27.8	0.7	3.5	17.1
Norway	7.5	10.0	28.3	0.1	4.6	11.2
Spain	12.5	8.8	28.7	4.0	10.7	27.3
Sweden	9.5	13.5	32.4	0.4	3.0	13.6
UK	17.5	7.0	57.7	1.0	12.7	52.3
United States	20.2	19.3	72.8	7.8	23.6	48.9

Double earnership has proliferated in most OECD countries, but single earnership remains quite widespread throughout Continental Europe, especially in the South. In Belgium, France, Germany and the Netherlands, about one in three working age couples still have to make ends meet on a single wage. For Italy and Spain this proportion is well over one in two. This is chiefly due to the comparatively low levels of female labour market participation in Continental Europe. In Spain and Italy, female employment rates remain well below 40 per cent. In most other Continental European countries, they tend not to exceed 55 per cent. By contrast, the female employment rates in the United States, Denmark, Norway and Sweden amount to around 70 per cent or more, and in Canada and the United Kingdom to around 65 per cent. A considerable proportion of female non-employment in Europe appears to be involuntary; female unemployment in the European Union reached almost 14 per cent in 1996 (OECD, 1997a).[3] It is possible, moreover, that unemployment, as measured by the standardized ILO definition, does not capture the real extent of involuntary non-employment among women. Many more may desire to work, even if they are not actively looking for a job.

Unemployment and especially non-employment rates are particularly high for women with lower levels of education. Non-employment rates for women with tertiary education are around 25 per cent in Belgium, France, Germany, Italy and the Netherlands. By contrast, non-employment rates for women with less than upper secondary education tend to be far higher: around 55 per cent for France, 60 per cent for Germany, 65 per cent for the Netherlands and around 70 per cent for Italy (OECD, 1997a).

The differential rise in double earnership may have given rise to a 'new' poverty risk: lack of a second household income. Let us look, therefore, at the incidence of relative poverty among single earner couples. For Belgium and the Netherlands we find poverty rates that are well below 5 per cent (Table 4.2). Couples having to make ends meet on a single wage face a slightly higher poverty risk (around 8 per cent) in France and Germany. Financial hardship among single earner couples appears to be more prevalent in Spain (10 per cent) and especially in Italy (14 per cent), where the breadwinner model remains far more dominant than in any of the other OECD countries included in this study.[4] Especially in the South, poverty at working age seems to be heavily concentrated among single earner households (Table 4.3).

Interestingly, there also appears to exist a relatively strong association between single earnership and poverty in the Anglo-Saxon countries.[5] We find poverty rates of around 13 per cent for single earner couples in Canada and the United Kingdom (Table 4.2). It seems that almost 25 per cent of single earner couples in the United States live in poverty. This is perhaps not surprising in one sense. One does, after all, expect to find higher poverty rates for single earner households in countries where low-wage work is more widespread, especially among 'male breadwinners'. The incidence of low-paid work among (prime-age) men is substantially higher in countries like the United States, Canada and the United Kingdom than in most Continental European countries (OECD, 1996). On the other hand, one would also expect that households in need of a second household income would find it easier to acquire this in the more flexible Anglo-Saxon labour markets, where low-paid jobs are more plentiful and labour market regulation less extensive. Double earnership *is* evidently more widespread in the Anglo-Saxon countries than in Continental Europe. Yet, we find that about one in four couples in Canada, the United Kingdom and the United States have to make ends meet on a single wage. In addition, OECD data suggest that less educated American or Canadian women are not more likely to be in work than those in France or Germany (OECD, 1997a).[6] Around 60 per cent of American women with less than upper secondary education are not in work. There is, moreover, evidence that, over the past two decades, female employment levels have increased most for (mostly well-educated) women living together with a partner with relatively high earnings (Juhn and Murphy, 1996). Labour market flexibility has, it appears, not prevented a growing gap.

Table 4.3:

The distribution of poor households with a working age head across various household types

	All	Single In work	Not in work	Two adult household Double earner	Single earner	No earner
Australia	100	17.2	47.1	3.0	11.9	20.8
Belgium	100	4.1	28.1	0.8	12.4	54.6
Canada	100	34.3	36.9	8.3	11.9	8.6
Denmark	100	53.4	37.8	2.6	3.0	3.2
Finland	100	58.8	30.0	6.1	2.1	3.0
France	100	8.8	43.6	1.0	24.6	21.9
Germany	100	27.2	38.2	5.1	16.2	13.3
Italy	100	1.5	8.8	2.4	56.1	31.2
Netherlands	100	29.0	40.9	2.6	12.3	15.2
Norway	100	60.6	31.8	0.7	5.4	1.5
Spain	100	6.9	16.4	5.7	46.1	25.0
Sweden	100	68.9	26.5	1.4	1.5	1.7
UK	100	7.8	49.2	2.1	13.6	27.2
United States	100	31.9	28.3	15.7	17.7	6.5

Workless Households and Poverty

Not surprisingly, we find the highest poverty rates for working-age households with no adult in work.[7] However, the extent of cross-national variation is quite striking (Table 4.2). Particularly eye-catching are the extremely high poverty rates for 'workless' one- and two-adult households in the Anglo-Saxon countries, where labour markets are most flexible and passive income support provisions least generous. The United States, for instance, has probably the most flexible labour market in the OECD area and people have, generally speaking, every incentive to work. The United States obviously enjoys a higher employment rate than most of the Continental European countries. However, non-employment rates for less educated Americans seem to be as high as elsewhere in the OECD area (OECD, 1997b), including many of the European countries where the less educated command much higher relative wages. In fact, there is evidence of a substantial rise in non-employment among less educated men, who have experienced dramatic real-wage decline over the past few decades (Freeman, 1995). It has been suggested that many have withdrawn from the labour market because the rewards from work have become too small. The comparatively high poverty rates for workless households in the United States - admittedly a rather heterogeneous group – seem to support the widely held view that there is a significant social cost attached to this apparent 'failure' of wage flexibility.

The United Kingdom has also become a major reference point in the debate about the potential social costs of labour market deregulation and wage flexibility. Enhanced wage flexibility and a tightening of benefits has apparently failed to bring down unemployment to satisfactory levels, especially among the least skilled. In fact, unemployment and non-employment rates for the less educated appear to be among the highest in the OECD area (OECD, 1997a; 1997b).[8] Even more striking is the fact that the proportion of 'workless households' soared during a period of labour market deregulation and widening wage disparities[9] (Gregg and Wadsworth, 1996). It is in this context worthwhile to draw attention to the comparatively high poverty rates for workless households in the United Kingdom, particularly for workless couples (Table 4.2).

4 LOW PAY AND POVERTY

Is 'Poverty in Work' Rampant in Countries Where Low Pay is More Prevalent ?

Keese and Swaim (1997) have demonstrated that employment rates for the most vulnerable groups in the labour market – women, youngsters and the low-skilled – do not tend to be consistently higher in countries where low-wage work is more prevalent. However, there does appear to be a fairly strong positive cross-country correlation between the incidence of low-wage employment among full-time workers, as reported by the OECD (1996), and the incidence of poverty among the working age population. As Figure 4.2 shows, countries like Finland, Sweden or Belgium, where less than one in ten full-time workers is low-paid, enjoy poverty rates of around 7 per cent or less. By contrast, countries like Canada, the UK or the United States, where about a fifth or more of the full-time workforce is low-paid, have poverty rates in

International Comparisons

the order of 15 per cent or more.

Figure 4.2
Low-wage employment and poverty

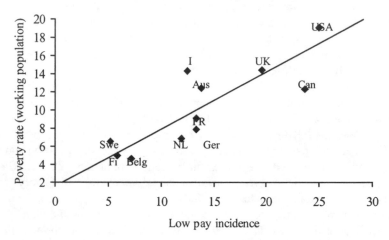

Rsq=0.7010
Source: Low Pay OECD (1996) estimates

The cross-country correlation between the incidence of low-paid work and poverty suggests that 'poverty in work' is more widespread in countries with a higher incidence of low-paid employment. This appears to be the case, but only to a limited extent. For the United States, where around a quarter of the full-time workforce is low-paid, we find a poverty rate of 14 per cent for those with some work attachment (Table 4.4) and a poverty rate of 7 per cent for full-year, full-time (FYFT) workers.[10] For Canada, however, where low pay is almost equally widespread, we find a poverty rate of less than 8 per cent for all workers and less than 3 per cent for FYFT workers. For the United Kingdom, where about a fifth of the full-time work force is low-paid, we find a poverty rate of just over 4 per cent for those with some work attachment and 3 per cent for those in FYFT work. Despite the high incidence of low pay in the United Kingdom, poverty at working age remains predominantly a problem associated with non-employment: about 75 per cent of poor households are 'workless households' (Table 4.3). For Germany and the Netherlands – both countries with a low-pay incidence of around 12 per cent – we find poverty rates of around 4 per cent for all workers and around 1 per cent for FYFT workers. Poverty rates for people in work are also very low in the Nordic countries, especially for prime-aged workers. Poverty appears virtually non-existent among FYFT workers in the Nordic countries.

Table 4.4:
Poverty rates for those in work

	All	By sex		By Age		
		Men	Women	-25	25-54	+55
Australia	5.4	4.6	6.5	9.7	4.1	3.8
Belgium	0.7	0.9	0.5	0.9	0.8	-
Canada	7.6	6.9	8.5	13.8	6.1	5.1
Denmark	2.8	2.5	3.1	8.9	1.3	0.6
Finland	3.9	3.4	4.3	12.3	1.8	1.3
France	3.1	3.1	3.0	5.1	2.7	3.8
Germany	4.4	4.1	4.9	9.7	3.9	3.5
Italy	6.3	8.7	2.1	5.5	6.4	6.8
Netherlands	3.8	3.1	5.0	11.1	2.1	1.6
Norway	3.2	2.7	3.6	8.3	1.9	0.5
Spain	7.1	7.4	6.5	6.7	7.1	8.2
Sweden	5.2	4.8	5.6	23.8	1.1	0.4
UK	4.1	3.2	5.1	3.7	4.3	3.3
United States	13.8	13.3	14.4	21.6	12.4	8.3

Low Pay and Poverty

We will now look in somewhat more detail at the link between low-wage work and poverty. Low-wage workers are defined here as full-year, full-time workers earning less than 66 per cent of the median gross wage of all full-year, full-time workers in that particular country. Since we measure poverty on the basis of disposable income over a whole year we also need to define 'low-pay' on a yearly basis. This means, unfortunately, that we cannot include low-paid temporary and part-time workers in the analysis. Note also that we cannot give estimates for countries for which there is no or insufficient information available on weeks and hours worked: Denmark, France, Italy, Norway and Spain. Let us also add that our estimates of the incidence of low-wage employment are for most countries broadly comparable to those made by Keese and Swaim (1997; OECD, 1996), who use a similar definition of low pay (see Table 4.A.2 in the Appendix). We obtain higher estimates for Belgium[11] and particularly for Sweden. These differences seem to be in part due to the fact that Keese and Swaim use country-specific definitions of what constitutes full-year, full-time work, while we use a single, relatively broad definition for all countries.

There is, apparently, only a relatively partial overlap between low pay and poverty (Table 4.5). The notable exception is the United States, where just about a quarter of the low-paid are in poverty. Poverty rates for low-paid FYFT workers are significantly lower for all the other countries for which we have data. The second highest poverty rate we find for Canada, where just over 10 per cent of low-paid workers are in poverty. For Australia, the Netherlands and the United Kingdom we find poverty rates for low-paid workers that are near to or below 10 per cent. For Belgium, Finland, Germany and Sweden we find poverty rates of around 5 per cent.

Table 4.5:
Poverty rates for low-paid FYFT workers

	All	By sex		By age		
		Men	Women	-25	25–54	+55
Australia	7.6	10.2	5.3	4.6	12.2	7.7
Belgium	6.2	16.1	1.6	1.5	8.6	0.0
Canada	11.5	13.7	9.8	8.9	12.5	9.3
Finland	4.3	7.4	3.0	3.6	4.9	0.0
Germany	5.6	7.5	4.3	3.6	6.7	0.0
Netherlands	9.5	12.8	6.0	4.8	17.7	0.0
Sweden	5.5	10.8	2.2	12.4	3.7	1.8
UK	8.8	13.0	5.6	4.2	13.3	6.8
United States	24.0	32.2	18.3	21.7	25.4	17.8

There is some variation by age. Poverty rates for prime-aged low-paid workers tend to be higher than those for young people working for low pay, except in Sweden. And as one would expect, the association between low pay and poverty is stronger for men than for women; poverty rates for low-paid men are typically twice as high as those for low-paid women (Table 4.5). In some countries, like Belgium or Sweden, the gender disparities seem to be even more significant. We need to point out, however, that our poverty estimates for some countries are based on relatively small samples of low-paid workers. The estimates which we present here should therefore be treated as indicative.

Most low-paid workers live in multi-earner households. This is certainly the case for low-paid women. The proportion of low-wage workers living in single-earner households varies from slightly over one in five in Canada and the United Kingdom to around one in three in Belgium and Germany (Table 4.6). In most countries, around 45 to 55 per cent of low wage workers live in double-earner households[12.] For Australia and the United Kingdom, we find that well over 30 per cent of low-paid workers live in a household with a least three earners, for Canada it is near to 30 per cent. For the other countries this proportion is considerably lower.

Table 4.6:

The distribution of low-paid FYFT workers by the number of earners in the household

	All		
	1 earner	2 earners	≥3 earners
Australia	24.3	39.3	36.4
Belgium	34.8	53.5	11.7
Canada	21.7	48.8	29.5
Finland	27.0	54.3	18.7
Germany	33.8	42.7	23.5
Netherlands	24.6	52.5	22.8
Sweden	28.5	67.7	3.8
UK	22.1	43.6	34.3
United States	28.1	49.5	22.4

	Men			Women		
	1 earner	2 earners	≥3 earners	1 earner	2 earners	≥3 earners
Australia	28.9	32.6	38.5	20.0	45.5	34.5
Belgium	42.5	40.5	17.0	31.2	59.6	9.3
Canada	23.9	43.2	32.9	20.2	52.7	27.1
Finland	31.5	45.5	23.0	25.1	57.9	16.9
Germany	51.1	27.0	21.9	28.0	48.1	24.0
Netherlands	29.1	43.5	27.4	19.8	62.4	17.9
Sweden	41.2	55.4	3.3	20.6	75.3	4.1
UK	28.0	36.0	36.0	17.7	49.3	33.0
United States	31.7	47.2	21.1	25.6	51.1	23.3

Low Pay and Poverty: To What Extent Does the Household Position of the Low-Paid Worker Matter ?

Generally speaking, there does not appear to be a very strong link between low pay and poverty. However, the poverty consequences of low pay are likely to be far more severe for households which have to make ends meet on a single wage. In effect, we find poverty rates of over 40 per cent for low-paid lone parents in Canada or the United States (Table 4.7). Unfortunately, due to insufficient sample size we are not able to give estimates for the other countries. As is evident from Table 4.8, lone parents make up only a fairly small fraction of the low-paid work force in most countries. (Recall that we are only considering here full-year, full-time employed low-paid workers.) Poverty rates for low-paid single-adult households without dependent children, who tend to make up a much larger fraction of the low-paid workforce (Table 4.8), are comparatively similar for most of the countries included in this study. We find poverty rates of slightly over 20 per cent for Canada, the United Kingdom and the United States and poverty rates of slightly below 20 per cent for the Netherlands and Sweden (Table 4.7).

We now turn our attention to couples. The poverty rates which we find for low-paid heads (always the male partner for purposes of comparability) tend to be quite considerable in most countries, especially when there are dependent children. The extent of cross-national variation is nevertheless striking. Our poverty estimates for low-paid men heading two-adult households with children range from well above 50 per cent in the United States to just above 5 per cent for Sweden. Apart from the United States, we find poverty rates of around or over 45 per cent for the United Kingdom and, perhaps somewhat surprisingly, the Netherlands. (But the estimate for the Netherlands is based on a rather small sample.) Poverty rates for low-paid men heading households with children are also quite considerable for Belgium (around 40 per cent), and Australia and Canada (around 30 per cent). We find comparatively low poverty rates for Germany (15 per cent), and especially for Finland (10 per cent) and Sweden (5 per cent). Poverty rates for low-paid men with a partner but no dependent children tend to be much lower in most countries. For the United States, we find a poverty rate of just under 20 per cent for childless couples with a low-paid head. The estimates we obtain for the other countries are considerably lower. It is interesting to note in this context that, for most countries, we find a relatively high proportion of low-paid men live together with a spouse who has no earnings or earnings from a part-time or temporary job (Table 4.9). Two notable exceptions are Finland and especially Sweden, where most low-paid men have a full-time employed spouse.

Table 4.7:
Poverty rates for low paid FYFT workers, for various household types

	Single		'Head' couple		'Spouse' couple	
	With children	No children	With children	No children	With children	No children
Australia	-	13.1	33.3	1.7	2.3	1.4
Belgium	-	-	(39.4)	-	0.0	0.0
Canada	41.7	20.3	27.2	8.0	6.0	1.2
Finland	-	10.4	(9.7)	(3.5)	1.3	0.5
Germany	-	(6.1)	16.1	1.5	0.0	0.6
Netherlands	-	(16.8)	(47.6)	(6.5)	-	3.3
Sweden	-	17.5	5.7	1.8	0.9	0.9
UK	-	21.6	45.6	10.3	4.6	3.4
United States	42.9	21.8	55.5	18.1	12.8	7.5

- denotes insufficient sample size (less than 25 unweighted observations); () denotes small sample size (between 25 and 50 unweighted observations)

Table 4.8:
The distribution of low-paid workers across various household types

	Single		'Head' couple		'Spouse' couple	
	With children	No children	With children	No children	With children	No children
Australia	4.2	22.0	18.8	11.8	22.7	20.4
Belgium	12.3	14.9	16.0	9.7	25.4	21.8
Canada	4.3	23.8	15.1	14.2	23.0	19.5
Finland	7.9	23.2	8.9	7.8	26.9	25.3
Germany	2.1	21.6	23.0	15.8	17.0	20.4
Netherlands	1.2	21.9	14.8	21.6	6.8	33.6
Sweden	5.3	23.5	12.8	11.9	32.1	14.3
UK	3.1	15.5	13.7	16.8	16.5	34.4
United States	11.2	20.5	19.4	12.0	19.7	17.2

Low-paid spouses – female partners in two-adult households – generally make up around 40 to 50 per cent of the low-paid workforce.[13] Poverty rates for this numerically important category of low-paid workers are very low in most countries, certainly when there are no dependent children. The United States is once again somewhat of an exception; we find a 13 per cent poverty rate for low-paid spouses with children. Poverty among low-paid spouses with dependent children also appears to be significant in Canada (6 per cent) and the United Kingdom (5 per cent). For the other countries included in this study we obtain estimates that are below 3 per cent.

Table 4.9:

Low-paid 'heads': the distribution of the employment status of the spouse

	FYFT employed, not low-paid	FYFT employed, low-paid	Temporary and/or part-time work	No earnings
Australia	14.7	8.1	42.3	35.0
Belgium	(11.6)	(8.4)	(15.5)	(64.5)
Canada	15.2	24.9	42.1	17.8
Finland	29.7	11.3	45.1	13.9
Germany	21.7	19.8	28.4	30.0
The Netherlands	13.1	16.9	38.7	31.3
Sweden	31.1	17.7	41.1	10.1
UK	9.3	16.8	36.7	37.7
United States	16.1	28.1	30.5	25.3

() denotes less than 50 unweighted cases

The Impact of Benefit and Tax Policies on Poverty: An Illustration

The purpose of this section is to illustrate that national tax and benefit policies appear to have a substantial impact on poverty rates for working age households. Table 4.10 shows pre-tax and pre-transfer poverty rates for all working age households in a selection of OECD countries. Poverty rates for households with a working age head, as calculated on the basis of pre-tax, pre-transfer income, are comparatively similar across countries.[14] They vary from 20 per cent to just over 25 per cent, except for Finland. The extent of cross-national variation in poverty rates becomes much more pronounced if social transfers are added in. Compare, for example, Belgium, Sweden and the United Kingdom, countries with similar pre-transfer, pre-tax poverty rates. When social transfers are added in, the poverty rate for Belgium drops to 5 per cent, for Sweden it drops to 8 per cent, and for the United Kingdom to 16 per cent. Social transfers seem to have much less of an impact on poverty in Canada and the United States. Personal taxes do not appear to have a particularly strong impact on poverty rates; for most countries, the poverty rate as calculated on the basis of disposable household income is only slightly higher than the poverty rate calculated on the basis of disposable household income before personal income taxes are paid.

Table 4.10:
Impact of social transfers and taxes on poverty rates:
all working age households

	Pre-transfer, pre-tax	Post-transfer, pre-tax	Post-transfer, post tax
Australia	20.1	13.6	14.5
Belgium	26.1	4.7	5.0
Canada	21.6	14.3	15.4
Finland	15.4	6.2	7.5
Germany	23.1	10.0	10.4
The Netherlands	21.1	5.3	8.3
Sweden	26.0	7.8	9.5
UK	26.0	16.3	17.5
United States	23.6	18.9	20.2

Let us now look at the impact of social transfers and personal taxes on poverty rates for low-paid households in various countries. We focus here on low-paid men heading a two-adult household with children (Table 4.11). The impact of social transfers on poverty appears to be massive in Sweden: the poverty rate drops from 35 per cent to less than 5 per cent if transfers are added in. Taxes appear to have a slightly negative impact, resulting in an effective poverty rate of around 6 per cent for low-paid heads with dependent children. The impact of transfers is less dramatic in Germany, but still very significant. The pre-transfer poverty rate drops from 37 per cent to 15 per cent when transfers are added in. As in Sweden, taxes have a slightly negative impact, resulting in a post-tax poverty rate of 16 per cent. Australia, too, has a pre-transfer, pre-tax poverty rate that is very similar to Sweden's. Social transfers, which are mostly means-tested, have a far more moderate impact on poverty; Australia's post-transfer poverty rate is 28 per cent. And taxes seem to have a stronger negative impact than in Germany or Sweden. We get a similar picture for Canada. Hence, the fact that Sweden's poverty rate for low-paid heads is 6 per cent, Germany's 16 per cent, Canada's 27 per cent

and Australia's 33 per cent seems to be largely due to the differential impact
of transfer and tax policies.

Table 4.11:
The impact of social transfers and taxes on poverty rates:
low-paid heads, couples with dependent children

	Pre-transfer pre-tax	Post-transfer, pre-tax	Post-transfer, post tax
Australia	38.5	27.5	33.3
Belgium	61.1	39.4	39.4
Canada	36.0	20.8	27.2
Germany	37.4	15.0	15.7
Sweden	34.7	4.0	5.7
UK	57.3	41.3	45.6
United States	57.1	50.2	55.5

The comparatively high poverty rates for low-paid heads with dependent
children in the United Kingdom and particularly the United States seem to be
related to the rather limited impact of social transfers and taxes on poverty.
Both for the United States and for the United Kingdom we find a pre-transfer,
pre-tax poverty rate of almost 60 per cent. If social transfers are added, the
poverty rate drops to around 40 per cent for the United Kingdom and 50 per
cent for the United States. However, taxes appear to have a comparatively
strong negative impact, resulting in a 45 per cent effective poverty rate for the
United Kingdom. The impact of social transfers is almost completely offset
by taxes in the United States; the effective poverty rate (55 per cent) is only
slightly lower than the pre-transfer, pre-tax rate.

5   POLICY CONCLUSIONS

Let us, before formulating a few tentative policy conclusions, summarize
some of the key findings. Perhaps the most striking finding is that poverty
rates for the working age population tend to be consistently higher in
countries where low-wage work is more prevalent. Countries like Finland,
Sweden or Belgium, where less than one in ten full-time workers is low-paid,
enjoy poverty rates of around 7 per cent or less. By contrast, countries like
Canada, the UK or the United States, where about a fifth or more of the full-
time workforce is low-paid, have poverty rates in the order of 15 per cent or

more. The relatively strong cross-country correlation between low pay and poverty suggests that 'poverty in work' is much more widespread in countries where low wage work is more prevalent. This appears to be the case, but only to a fairly limited extent. Few advanced countries, with the possible exception of the United States are confronted with rampant "poverty in work', even countries where a fairly large fraction of the workforce is low-paid, like in Canada or the United Kingdom. In addition, poverty rates for low-paid workers are well below 10 per cent in most of the countries included in this study, except in the United States, where about a quarter of low-paid workers are confronted with poverty. However, much depends on the household status of the low-paid worker. Low-paid 'breadwinners' tend to face a substantial poverty risk, especially in countries with less extensive benefit systems. By contrast, poverty rates for secondary earners – who typically make up the majority of the low-paid workforce – tend to be almost insignificant in most of the countries included in this study. In fact, poverty rates for households with a low wage as a second household income tend to be lower than for households which have to make ends meet on a single earned income.

Should high-unemployment Continental Europe dispose of at least some of the barriers to low-wage employment? Policy makers seem to be faced with something of a dilemma. Unemployment and certainly non-employment rates remain high, particularly for less educated women. It is reasonable to assume that many of them seek to acquire a (modest) second household income, rather than full financial independence. Moreover, our findings suggest that double earnership is almost a watertight guarantee against poverty at working age. It is sometimes argued that an expansion of low-wage employment would make it easier for single-earner households to acquire a second income. While an expansion of low-wage work may improve the job prospects of less educated women it also entails the risk of increasing or intensifying financial hardship among households having to make ends meet on a single wage – single persons and single parents – and single earner couples who fail to secure a second income. As we have seen, poverty rates for single earner households tend to be substantially higher in countries where low-wage work is more prevalent. Moreover, employment rates for less educated women do not tend to be consistently higher in countries where low-wage work is more prevalent.

The more contentious policy question is, however, whether labour markets ought to be deregulated *and* benefits tightened in order to encourage, if not force, the unemployed living on benefits to move out of passive dependence and into work. It is often argued that emphasis ought to be shifted from passive benefit support to in-work benefits and wage supplements. The idea is to make work more attractive and to prevent poverty in work. The argument in favour of less generous 'passive' benefits and more generous in-work benefits is appealing in many respects. A major problem is, however, that low-wage supplements and other work-related provisions would offer no income protection at all to those who see their benefit reduced or taken away altogether but who fail to secure even a low-paid job. The experience in a number of countries suggests that this problem is not hypothetical; even countries with highly flexible labour markets and comparatively non-generous 'passive' benefits for the unemployed have failed to eradicate unemployment among the least skilled. Some of the evidence presented here suggests that there may be a significant social cost attached to this apparent 'failure' of labour market flexibility.

APPENDIX 4.A: DATA AND DEFINITIONS

Data For our analysis we used the datasets listed in Table 4.A1, as compiled, standardized and made available by remote access by the Luxembourg Income Study. For a full description of the datasets and the standardization procedure we refer to Atkinson, Rainwater and Smeeding (1995) and to the LIS information packages (http://lissy.ceps.lu). For an assessment of data quality we refer to Atkinson *et al.* (1995; appendix 4) and to Cantillon *et al.* (1997).

Table 4.A.1:
Luxembourg Income Study datasets

Country	Year	Name of LIS Survey	Period	Unit of measure-ment
Australia	1989	Australian Income and Housing Survey	Year	Household
Belgium	1992	Centre of Social Policy Panel Survey	Month	Household
Canada	1991	Survey of Consumer Finances	Year	Household
Denmark	1992	Income Tax Survey	Year	Household
Finland	1991	Income Distribution Survey	Year	Household
France	1989	Household Budget Survey	Year	Household
Germany	1994	Socio-Economic Panel	Year	Household
Italy	1991	Bank of Italy Income Survey	Year	Household
Netherlands	1991	Socio-Economic Panel CBS	Year	Household
Norway	1991	Income and Property Distribution Survey	Year	Household
Spain	1990	Family Expenditure Survey	Year	Household
Sweden	1992	Income Distribution Survey	Year	Tax Unit
United Kingdom	1991	Family Expenditure Survey	Year	Family
United States	1991	March Current Population Survey	Year	Household

Table 4.A.2:
Incidence of low pay among FYFT workers (LIS based estimates)

	All	By sex			By age		
		Men	Women	-25	25–54	+55
Australia	14.5	10.4	22.4	40.7	7.8	5.9
Belgium	10.8	5.1	22.3	19.8	9.1	15.3
Canada	21.4	15.0	30.7	50.3	18.3	18.9
Finland	6.7	3.8	9.6	26.9	5.6	4.8
Germany	12.7	7.9	22.5	33.1	11.8	9.7
Netherlands	12.4	8.1	30.0	62.5	5.6	3.6
Sweden	11.2	6.9	18.3	26.5	9.5	10.0
UK	19.9	12.7	34.4	46.9	13.1	18.2
United States	26.4	19.0	36.3	63.5	22.9	21.0

Definition of employment and low-wage employment Poverty is measured on the basis of household income over the whole year (only the Belgian data cover one month). 'Employment' and 'non-employment' are therefore also measured on a yearly basis. 'Non-employed' are those with zero annual labour earnings in the reference year, with consistency checks on the available labour force status variables. 'Employed' are those with non-zero annual labour earnings. The self-employed are excluded from our analysis.

Those with a missing value on the wage variable are also excluded from the analysis (a substantial share only in the case of Germany). Full-year, full-time workers are workers who work 44 weeks or more per year, and more than 33 hours per week. Low-paid workers are workers who work full-year, full-time and who earn less than 66 per cent of the median gross wage for full-year, full-time workers.

NOTES

1. The working age population comprises all individuals between the age of 16 and 64.
2. A double-earner household refers to the fact that both partners have some labour income during the reference year. Dependent children in work or third persons are not taken into account.
3. There is, however, a considerable degree of cross-national variation. Female unemployment

4. rates range from well below 10 per cent in Denmark, the Netherlands, Sweden and the United Kingdom to almost 30 per cent in Spain.

4. Family solidarity is widely thought to act as a substitute for underdeveloped public provisions. Poverty in the South may be overestimated if family solidarity is more extensive than elsewhere in the OECD, and if transfers within the (extended) family are not adequately measured.

5. We also find comparatively high poverty rates (around 10 per cent) for single-person households with labour earnings in the Scandinavian countries. The vast majority are young people living alone, presumably many of them students. It is also useful to point out that in the case of Sweden all children over the age of 18 are treated as economically independent – whether they actually are or not – in the survey on which these estimates are based.

6. 'Less educated' refers to those who have not completed an upper secondary education. A smaller proportion of the labour force is 'less educated' in Canada or the United States than in most other industrialized countries (OECD, 1995). However, it appears that a similar picture would emerge if one would compare unemployment and non-employed rates for the bottom 20 per cent of the labour force ranked by educational attainment (OECD, 1997b).

7. Excluding 'third' adult persons living in the household.

8. The less educated constitute a fairly large section of the population at working age in the United Kingdom. Around one third of the population at working age has a level of education below upper secondary education, as compared to less than one in five in the United States or Germany (OECD, 1995).

9. The incidence of low-wage employment crept up from just over 15 per cent during the late 70s to almost 20 per cent in the mid 90s (Keese and Swaim, 1997).

10. See Appendix for the definition of 'workers' and full-year, full-time (FYFT) workers. We do not give the table for FYFT workers because the picture is virtually identical to the one provided by Table 4.4.

11. The Belgian income data cover one month in 1992. A FYFT worker refers in the case of Belgium to a full-time worker, i.e. a person employed for more than 33 hours per week.

12. A notable exception is Sweden, where almost 70 per cent of low-wage workers live in a double-earner household. This is probably related to the fact that the Swedish survey assumes all persons over the age of 18 to be economically independent. Therefore, the share of low-wage workers living in households with three earners or more is also much lower in Sweden than elsewhere.

13. Low-paid FYFT children living in the parental home are not included in this table.

14. Property and wealth taxes and indirect taxes are not taken into account. Mandatory social security contributions are also not included because the relevant information is not available for most countries. Social transfers refer to all public sector cash transfers, including child and family allowances.

REFERENCES

Atkinson, A.B. (1995), *Incomes and the Welfare State*, Cambridge University Press.

Atkinson, A., Rainwater, L. and Smeeding, T. (1995), *Income Distribution in OECD Countries*, Paris: OECD.

Callan, T. and Nolan, B. (1991), Concepts of Poverty and the Poverty Line, *Journal of Economic Surveys*, vol. 5 no. 3, pp. 243–261.

Cantillon, B., Marx, I. and Van den Bosch, K. (1997), The Challenge of Poverty and Social Exclusion, in OECD, *Family, Market and Community: Equity and Efficiency in Social Policy*, Paris: OECD.

Duncan, G., Gustafsson, B., Hauser, R., Schmaus, G., Jenkins, S., Messinger, Social Assistance in the United States, Canada, and Europe, in K. McFate, Lawson, R. and Wilson W.J. (1995), *Poverty, inequality and the future of social protection*, Russell Sage Foundation, New York.

European Commission (1996), *Employment in Europe*, Brussels.

Freeman, R. (1995), The Limits of Wage Flexibility to Curing Unemployment, *Oxford Review of Economic Policy*, 11 (1): 63–72.

Gregg, P. and Wadsworth, J. (1996), More Work in Fewer Households?, in Hills, J. (ed), *New Inequalities: The Changing Distribution of Income and Wealth in the UK*, Cambridge University Press, Cambridge.

Jenkins, S. (1991), Poverty Measurement and the Within-Household Distribution: Agenda for Action, *The Journal of Social Policy*, vol. 20, nr. 4, pp. 457–483.

Juhn, C. and Murphy, K. (1996), Wage Inequality and Family Labour Supply, NBER Working Paper # 5459, Cambridge (MA): NBER.

Keese, P. and Swaim, M. (1997): *The Incidence and Dynamics of Low-Wage Employment in OECD countries*, Paper presented at the European Low-Wage Employment Research Network Conference on the Problems of Low-Wage Employment, 31 January – 1 February, Bordeaux.

OECD (1995), *Education at a Glance*, Paris: OECD.

OECD (1996), *Employment Outlook*, Paris: OECD.

OECD (1997a), *Employment Outlook*, Paris: OECD.

OECD (1997b), *Policies for Low-paid Workers and Unskilled Job Seekers*, Paris: OECD.

Van den Bosch, K., Callan, T., Estivill, J., Hausman, P., Jeandidier, B., Muffels, R. and Yfantopoulos, J. (1993), A Comparison of Poverty in Seven European Countries and Regions using Subjective and Relative Measures, *Journal of Population Economics,* vol. 6, pp. 235–259.

PART TWO

Individual Country Experiences

5. Low Pay, the Earnings Distribution and Poverty in Ireland, 1987-1994

Brian Nolan

1   INTRODUCTION

Sharply rising inequality in the overall earnings distribution and increased returns to education and skills have been identified in a number of industrialised countries, notably the USA and the UK. Other industrialised countries have seen a much less pronounced rise in dispersion, if any, and institutional differences such as the extent of collective bargaining and wage regulation may be important influences (see OECD 1993, 1996). The links between such trends in the earnings distribution and the extent of low pay, and between low pay and household poverty, are of immediate concern for policy makers. However, there are major gaps in our understanding of these links, and the aim of this chapter is to investigate them with data for Ireland.

A detailed picture of the extent and nature of low pay in Ireland in 1987 and its relationship with household poverty, based on analysis of a large-scale household survey carried out by the ESRI, was presented in Nolan (1993). In 1994 another large-scale survey has been carried out, the first wave of the Irish element of the European Community Household Panel, obtaining *inter alia* detailed information on earnings, education and experience for about 3,500 employees. In this chapter these data are used to compare the overall distribution of earnings, the extent and incidence of low pay, and the relationship between low pay and household poverty, in 1987 and 1994. This allows Ireland to be added to the available observations on recent trends in earnings inequality in industrialised countries, and points towards fruitful approaches to analysing the relationship between individual low pay and household poverty, using both monetary and non-monetary indicators of poverty and social exclusion.

The chapter is structured as follows. Section 2 describes the Irish background and the data employed. Section 3 examines trends in the earnings distribution between 1987 and 1994. Section 4 focuses on the extent of low pay and the characteristics of those affected. Section 5 describes the extent and nature of household poverty and Section 6 deals with the relationship between low pay and household poverty. Section 7 summarises the conclusions.

2   BACKGROUND AND DATA

The central feature of the Irish economy during the period being studied here is exceptionally strong economic growth. In each of the years from 1987 to 1994 growth in real Gross Domestic Product exceeded both the European Union and OECD average, and in the 1990s Ireland has been one of the fastest growing economies in either grouping. This marks a significant turn-around from the prolonged recession experienced in Ireland in the early and mid-1980s, when the impact of global recession was exacerbated by the need to rein in public sector borrowing and debt after injudicious pump-priming of the economy at the end of 1970s. The high public sector deficits of that period have been eliminated, and both the balance of trade and the overall current account balance moved into strong surplus. This 'Celtic Tiger' appears to be driven by the coincidence of several favourable factors rather than any single one in isolation, with the candidates ranging from the tightening of fiscal policy in the 1980s, centralised wage-bargaining, improvements in competitiveness, inflow of EU structural funds, and the increasing level of educational qualifications and skills.[1]

Here our concern is with the labour market. Having been far worse than the EU average during 1981–86, Ireland's performance in increasing employment levels has been better than in the EU-12 or even the USA. However a legacy of the prolonged recession of the early and mid-1980s was a very high rate of unemployment, peaking at 17.6% of the labour force in 1987. This remained stubbornly high during the period 1987–94 despite strong economic growth, though it had fallen to 15.6% by 1994 (and has subsequently fallen more rapidly to below the EU average). This was partly because out-migration was low in the latter half of the period due to the improved situation in the domestic labour market and deterioration in the UK.

During this period Ireland has operated a social partnership approach between the state, employers, unions and farming interests. Since 1987, successive national agreements have formalized a consensus between the social partners on not only pay increases but also on the strategic direction for the public finances, as well as commitment to reduce unemployment, reduce the tax burden on employees, introduce employment legislation, combat social exclusion, etc.[2] The contribution of these agreements to Ireland's rapid economic growth, and indeed the extent to which they represent successful social corporatism, is debated (see for example Teague 1995, Sexton and O'Connell 1997) but they clearly played the central role in wage determination.

Another key feature of the Irish labour market during the period being studied is the very substantial increase in the supply of skilled labour. This reflects increasing educational participation rates in the preceding years, with roots going back as far as the introduction of free secondary education in the late 1960s, constituting an 'educational revolution' (Fahey and FitzGerald 1997). Comparative data compiled by the OECD (1996) from the mid-1980s show participation in third-level education expanding more rapidly in Ireland than in most other European Union countries. Over that period 1985–94 the proportion of those aged 18–21 enrolled in tertiary education doubled in the Irish case, and the proportion of 16–17 year-olds still in education was also relatively high.[3] This enhancement in the levels of educational attainment of those entering the labour force in the 1980s and 1990s, together with the exit from the labour force of older age groups with much lower levels of attainment, is reflected in a relatively rapid change in the educational profile of employees between 1987 and 1994.

Turning to a description of the data to be employed in this chapter, these come from two large-scale household surveys carried out by the Economic and Social Research Institute. The first is the survey of income distribution, poverty and usage of State services carried out in 1987, which obtained responses from a sample of 3,294 households, with a response rate of 64% of valid addresses contacted. The sampling frame was the Register of Electors and the survey was designed to provide a national sample from the population resident in private households. The sample has been reweighted to correct for non-response, on the basis of four variables – number of adults in the household, urban/rural location, age and socio-economic group of household head – using external information from the much larger Labour Force Survey. The representativeness of this sample data has been validated by comparison with a variety of external information, and it has been used extensively in research on poverty and tax and social welfare policy in Ireland. (A full description of the survey is in Callan, Nolan *et al.,* 1989, and an overview of that research is in Nolan and Callan eds. 1994). Information on earnings, education, labour market experience and other characteristics of 2,700 employees in sample households was obtained. This appears to represent employees well when compared with available data from the Census of Population and the Labour Force Survey, and has served as the basis for an in-depth analysis of the extent and nature of low pay in Ireland at that date (Nolan 1993), as well as research on the determinants of individual earnings and on male–female wage differentials.[4] Comparable micro-data for earlier years are not available for analysis, but on the basis of the limited published results the 1987 figures did not appear to show a marked increase in earnings dispersion since 1979–80.

The more recent source of data on earnings and poverty is the 1994 Living in Ireland Survey, the first wave of the Irish element of the European Community Household Panel (ECHP) being carried out for Eurostat by the ESRI. This obtained information for 4,048 households, a response rate of 62.5% of valid addresses contacted; once again the Electoral Register was the sampling frame and the responses were reweighted to accord with the Labour Force Survey in terms of key household characteristics. First results from this survey on household poverty have just been published in Callan *et al.* (1996), which also contains a comprehensive description of the survey itself. This chapter analyses the individual earnings of employees in the 1994 sample and the relationship between low pay and household poverty. The sample contains 3,412 individual employees who responded fully to questions about their earnings and hours of work, occupation, labour market experience, and education. As in the 1987 ESRI survey, employees were asked about the gross pay they received in their last pay period, and about how long this covered (week, fortnight, month etc.) and the hours worked during that period. They were also asked whether this was the amount they usually receive, and if not, what was their usual gross pay and hours usually worked. In looking at the distribution of earnings and the extent of low pay, for the 5% of respondents who stated that their last pay was not usual we use the amount usually received, and for the remaining 95% we use current weekly reported gross pay.

3   THE DISTRIBUTION OF EARNINGS

In looking at the distribution of earnings across individuals, it is customary to focus on either hourly earnings, or on weekly earnings for full-time employees only. In the Irish case 18 hours per week is the statutory cut-off for social insurance purposes, and about 7% of employees in 1994 worked less than this, up from 4% in 1987. We therefore look at both the distribution of hourly earnings among all the employees in our samples, and at the distribution of weekly earnings among those working 18 hours or more per week. Table 5.1 shows the distribution of gross hourly and weekly earnings in Ireland in 1987 and 1994 on this basis, as measured by the bottom decile, bottom quartile, top quartile and top decile as percentages of the median. We see that from 1987 to 1994 there was a consistent widening in dispersion for both weekly and hourly earnings, particularly at the top of the distribution. In the case of weekly earnings the top decile rose from 184% to 196% of the median, and for hourly earnings the increase was from 196% to 224%.

This widening in dispersion is not attributable simply to changing numbers of male versus female or 'young' versus adult employees. Table 5.2

shows that a sharp widening took place between 1987 and 1994 in the distribution of hourly earnings among men only, and also among full-time adult (21 years or over) men. Indeed, the fall in the bottom decile as a percentage of the median is considerably larger when one concentrates on men only than it was for the distribution as a whole.

Table 5.1:

Distribution of earnings, Ireland 1987 and 1994

As proportion of median	1987	1994
All employees, hourly earnings:		
Bottom decile	0.47	0.47
Bottom quartile	0.73	0.68
Top quartile	1.37	1.50
Top decile	1.96	2.24
Full-time employees, weekly earnings:		
Bottom decile	0.45	0.43
Bottom quartile	0.72	0.68
Top quartile	1.39	1.43
Top decile	1.84	1.96

Table 5.2:

Distribution of hourly earnings among men, Ireland 1987 and 1994

As proportion of median	1987	1994
Hourly earnings: all male employees:		
Bottom decile	0.53	44.9
Bottom quartile	0.76	69.8
Top quartile	1.35	147.6
Top decile	1.86	222.6
Hourly earnings: full-time adult male employees:		
Bottom decile	0.62	0.55
Bottom quartile	0.77	0.74
Top quartile	1.34	1.44
Top decile	1.84	2.09

4   LOW PAY IN IRELAND 1987 AND 1994

A variety of approaches can be used to define and measure low pay, and these will not be reviewed here (see for example CERC 1991, OECD 1996; Nolan 1993 discusses approaches previously applied to Irish data). The method which appears most likely to permit cross-country comparisons is to adopt the low pay cut-off employed by the OECD in its recent study, of two-thirds of median earnings, and in addition to apply the more stringent criterion of half median earnings to allow the sensitivity of the results to the choice of cut-off to be seen. The OECD study defined low-paid workers as full-time workers who earn less than two-thirds of the median weekly earnings for full-time workers. (This was not always the basis on which the country results it presents were produced, however, as discussed below.) Here we also apply the half median weekly earnings criterion to full-time workers, and in addition apply both two-thirds and half the median for hourly earnings for all employees. Table 5.3 shows the results for 1987 and 1994.

Table 5.3:
Extent of low pay in Ireland, 1987 and 1994

% below:	1987	1994
Full-time employees:		
50% of median weekly earnings	12.1	13.4
66% of median weekly earnings	20.7	23.6
All employees:		
50% of median hourly earnings	11.0	11.4
66% of median hourly earnings	19.9	23.0

We see that in 1987 21% of full-time employees had weekly gross earnings below the OECD's two-thirds of the median low pay cut-off. Using half the median as cut-off would identify about one in eight as low paid in weekly terms in 1987. The corresponding hourly cut-offs for all employees identify a slightly lower percentage as low paid in each case. By 1994, the percentage below half median earnings was little changed but with the two-thirds cut-off had risen, with the percentage of full-time employees with weekly earnings below the two-thirds cut-off up from 21% to 23%.

International comparisons of the extent of low pay are problematic because of differences in methods, coverage, definitions etc. Here we simply reproduce the results for a range of other OECD countries in 1993–1995 presented in OECD (1996), which in principle refer to the percentage of full-time workers below two-thirds of median weekly earnings. In fact, the results for some countries refer to annual earnings or to hourly earnings, some cover only year-round full-time workers, some cover only certain sectors, and some are net rather than gross earnings (see Annex 3A, OECD 1996 for detailed definitions for each country). While highlighting the limitations of what is possible with currently available data, it is none the less useful to employ these figures to provide some comparative context for the Irish results. We see that on this basis Ireland in 1994 has one of the highest levels of low pay of the OECD countries covered. The only country with more than Ireland's 24% below the OECD benchmark is the USA with 25%, while Canada has a figure very close to Ireland's and the UK is at 20%. Most of the other countries shown are below 15%.

Table 5.4:

Extent of low pay in Ireland 1994 compared with other OECD countries

% full-time employees below 66% of median weekly earnings:	Around 1994[a]
Ireland	23.6
Australia	13.8
Austria	13.2
Belgium	7.2
Canada	23.7
Finland	5.9
France	13.3
Germany	13.3
Italy	12.5
Japan	15.7
Netherlands	11.9
New Zealand	16.9
Sweden	5.2
Switzerland	13.0
United Kingdom	19.6
United States	25.0

[a] Results for Ireland are for 1994, and for other countries are 1993, 1994 or 1995.
Source: OECD (1996) Table 3.2 p. 72.

Table 5.5:
Low pay by age and sex, Ireland 1994

% below 2/3 median:	Risk			Composition		
Age	Male	Female	All	Male	Female	All
Under 25	59.4	62.4	60.8	28.6	26.8	55.4
25-35	11.5	23.7	16.7	8.2	12.9	21.0
35-45	4.4	26.2	11.5	3.1	8.7	11.8
45-55	3.9	30.5	11.8	1.9	6.4	8.3
55 +	7.3	24.5	12.3	1.4	2.0	3.4
All	16.7	35.6	23.6	43.3	56.7	100.0

Note: Full-time employees only, weekly earnings.

Table 5.6:
Low pay by occupational group, Ireland 1994
% below 2/3 median

Occupational Group:	Risk	Composition
Agricultural workers	64.8	7.0
Producers, makers and repairers	21.8	19.8
Labourers and unskilled workers (not elsewhere specified)	35.5	6.7
Transport, communications and storage workers	17.2	5.3
Clerical workers	20.6	13.6
Commerce, insurance and finance	48.0	20.2
Service workers	43.2	20.2
Professional and technical workers	8.0	6.4
Others (administrative, executive and managerial workers)	2.7	0.9
All	23.6	100.0

The variation in the risk of low pay in Ireland by age, sex and occupation, and the composition of the low paid in those terms, may be briefly examined. The results presented are for full-time workers below two-thirds of the median, but a similar pattern of variation is seen with the alternative weekly or hourly thresholds. Table 5.5 shows that the probability of being low paid for women is about twice that for men overall, but that most of this differential is among those aged 25 or over. The percentage low paid is very much higher among those aged under 25 than among older workers. In terms of composition, about 55% of the low paid are aged under 25, 30% are women aged 25 or over, and 15% are men aged 25 or over.

Table 5.6 shows enormous variation in the percentage of low paid across broad occupational groups (using broad groupings employed by the Irish Central Statistics Office in the annual Labour Force Survey). The risk of being low paid reaches almost two-thirds for employees in agriculture, is also relatively high for labourers and those working in commercial and service occupations, and is very low for those in professional or technical and administrative/managerial occupations.

5 HOUSEHOLD POVERTY AND EARNINGS

To examine the relationship between low pay and poverty, we must first specify how 'the poor' are to be defined and measured. The definition of poverty which appears to be widely, though by no means universally, accepted in industrialised countries refers to exclusion from the ordinary life of the community due to lack of resources. Even among those adopting this definition, there is no consensus about how best to measure poverty. We follow the general approach advocated by Atkinson (1985, 1987) and Foster and Shorrocks (1988), acknowledging the diversity of possible judgements about the specification of the poverty line and choice of poverty measure and taking this into account in the measurement procedures adopted. We begin by deriving a set of relative income poverty lines, of the type employed *inter alia* in recent studies for the European Commission, Eurostat and the OECD (O'Higgins and Jenkins 1989, ISSAS 1990, Hagenaars, de Vos and Zaidi, *et al.* 1994, Forster 1994), and in cross-country comparisons based on the Luxembourg Income Study data such as Buhman *et al.* (1988).[5] (This approach is compared with other methods of deriving poverty lines in Callan and Nolan, 1991.) These relative lines are simply calculated as a proportion of mean or median income. While both are used, unlike the low-pay literature, poverty studies tend to use the mean more often than the median. For this reason we follow the most common practice of using 50% and 60% of mean household equivalent income as the relative income poverty thresholds, corresponding to the most commonly-quoted poverty studies such as those carried out for the EU, for whom 'half average income' has been an easily understood poverty standard. (Median-based relative lines produce very much the same pattern in terms of the low pay/household poverty overlap.)

The equivalence scales employed may have a significant impact on the size and composition of the group falling below the poverty line (Buhman *et al* 1988, Coulter, Cowell and Jenkins 1992), and no method of deriving such scales commands general support. (Varying the scale will alter not only the relative position of households of different size and composition but also the level of average equivalent income across all households, and thus the level of the poverty lines themselves.) The set of scales employed here is based on those implicit in the Irish social welfare system's rates of support in 1987: where the household head is 1, each extra adult is 0.66 and each child is 0.33. Alternative scales have also been employed with the 1987 sample and produced similar results in terms of the extent of income poverty and the overlap between low pay and poverty (see Callan and Nolan 1992, Nolan 1993).

In measuring poverty the income concept used is disposable income, that is gross income minus income tax and social security contributions. Total income from all sources must now be taken into account, and the period over which these are measured is important. Here employee earnings, private pensions and social security transfers are measured for the previous week (or month for monthly paid employees or pensioners), while the more variable self-employment and investment income are measured over a longer period, usually a year. The recipient unit used in measuring poverty is generally either the household or the narrower nuclear family/tax unit of single person or couple together with dependent children. As with the choice of equivalence scale, there is little basis on which to say that one is preferable to the other – this may depend on the degree of income sharing within the units and the particular problem to be analyzed - and yet the results obtained may differ. Here we adopt the more common approach of using the household; results for 1987 reported in Nolan (1993) show that the overlap between low pay and poverty in the Irish case is not in fact affected significantly by the choice of unit. Using the household or family as recipient unit involves the conventional assumption, explicit or implicit, that resources are shared within the household/family so as to equalize living standards. This assumption has been questioned, but the intra-household distribution is not an issue which we address here (though see Cantillon and Nolan 1998 for an analysis based on non-monetary deprivation indicators).

Table 5.7 shows the percentage of households falling below these relative income poverty lines in 1987 and 1994, using the household as recipient unit and the 1/0.66/0.33 equivalence scale. The choice of relative income cut-off clearly makes a great difference to the percentage of households in poverty, which ranges from 18% to 35% in 1994. An increase in the percentage of households below each of the relative income lines between 1987 and 1994 is seen (though the extent to which the income of these households falls below the lines has in fact fallen sharply, as analyzed in detail in Callan *et al.* 1996).

Table 5.7:
Households in poverty, Ireland 1987 and 1994

% of households below:	1987	1994
50% of mean equivalent income	16.3	18.5
60% of mean equivalent income	28.5	34.6

Table 5.8:
Households below relative income lines by labour force status of head,
Ireland 1987 and 1994

Labour force status of head	1987		1994	
Labour force status	Below 50% income line	Below 60% income line	Below 50% income line	Below 60% income line
Employee	8.2	13.4	6.2	8.0
Self-employed	4.8	4.4	6.7	4.7
Farmer	23.7	17.5	8.9	7.7
Unemployed	37.4	26.6	32.6	23.7
Ill/Disabled	11.1	13.1	9.5	7.0
Retired	8.1	9.4	10.5	20.6
Home Duties	6.7	15.6	25.5	28.2
All	100.0	100.0	100.0	100.0

How many of these low-income households rely on earnings as their main income source? Table 5.8 shows the households below these relative lines classified by the labour force status of the household head. In 1987, 8% of the households below half mean income, and 13% of those below the 60% line, were headed by an employee. Those below the relative lines were dominated by two groups: households headed by an unemployed person and those headed by a farmer, accounting for about 60% of all households below half mean income. By 1994, households headed by a farmer comprised a much smaller proportion of those below the relative lines, but had been 'replaced' by households headed by someone who is retired or 'in home duties' -

working full-time in the home. Households headed by an employee still only accounted for 6–8% of those below the relative income lines. This comes about because, although households headed by an employee account for 38% of the sample, they face a very low risk of being in poverty: in 1994, only 3% of such households are below half mean income and 8% are below the 60% line, marginally down from 1987 and much lower than the risk-facing households not headed by an employee.

Focusing simply on the household head could understate the importance of earnings since households below the relative lines could still contain other members who are employees. In fact, in 1994 only about 12% of households below half mean income and 15% of those below the 60% line contain an employee (whether the head or not).[6] Using the family rather than the household as recipient unit once again does not significantly increase the importance of earnings from employment for those below relative income lines.

The low-income population in Ireland is thus currently dominated by households relying primarily on social security transfers, and to a much more limited extent self-employment income or occupational pensions, rather than employee earnings. Income from self-employment is however known to be difficult to measure in household surveys, and farm income poses particular problems. Further, it may be the case that because farm incomes are more variable from year to year than other income sources, those relying on it tend to smooth consumption and would not therefore be so severely affected by one bad year.[7] It could be the case, then, that focusing on current income gives a misleading picture of the living standards of households relying on income from different sources. A combination of understatement of income from self-employment in surveys and greater smoothing by those receiving it could lead to an overestimate of the importance of households relying on self-employment income among the poor. It is also sometimes argued that those relying on social security transfers are in some respects better off than those at similar income levels but receiving earnings, because the former do not incur travel to work and other work-related expenses and because they may receive more non-cash benefits in the form of free or subsidized goods and services. It could be the case, then, that comparisons simply on the basis of current disposable income overstate the relative position of households relying on earnings relative to other households, and underestimate their importance among the poor. Finally, even if this were not the case, current income alone has limitations as an indicator of exclusion due to lack of resources, for reasons discussed at length elsewhere (e.g. Nolan and Whelan 1996) .

For all these reasons, it is worth trying to go beyond income poverty lines in assessing the relative living standards of those relying on earnings. To do so, we employ indicators of deprivation, selected from a wider set of items and activities on which information was obtained in our survey. A full description of the way these have been derived and used is given in Callan, Nolan and Whelan (1993) and Nolan and Whelan (1996) and only the briefest summary is possible here. Drawing on Townsend (1979) and Mack and Lansley (1985), information was sought in the surveys on whether respondents had/did a range of items or activities, whether they regarded them as necessities, and for those who did not have/do a particular item/activity, whether they had to do without due to lack of money. The items/activities covered everyday consumption items such as having meat/fish regularly, more irregular items such as clothes, shoes, and holidays, durables such as a TV, car and washing machine, and housing-related items such as having an indoor toilet and a bath/shower. Using information of this sort, previous studies have generally selected as deprivation indicators the sub-set possessed by most households or regarded as necessities by most people, and constructed a summary deprivation index. Scores for each item may be based simply on absence, or may take into account whether this is said to be due to lack of money, perhaps also using income to assess whether absence is 'enforced'. However, constructing a summary index across items in this way implicitly assumes a single underlying dimension of deprivation, whereas exploring the relationship between the indicators may be helpful.

Factor analysis in fact reveals that the items on which we have information cluster into three distinct groups. The first contains items relating to 'basic life-style deprivation' – absence of rather basic consumption items such as food, clothing and heating. The second mostly refers to absence of leisure activities such as hobbies or evenings out, holidays, presents. The third group consists of items related to housing and household capital items, such as damp-free dwelling, toilet and bath/shower, washing machine and fridge. This suggests that it is useful to distinguish these three dimensions rather than simply adding items across dimensions in a summary index. While they could be used in various ways, here we concentrate on the first group or dimension, of what we have termed 'basic' deprivation indicators. These items are both regarded as necessities and possessed by most people in the samples, in contrast with the second group which are not actually possessed by most households and are not overwhelmingly regarded as necessities. The housing items are possessed by most people and regarded as necessities by almost everyone, but their absence does not appear to be particularly strongly related to current resources, with age, household composition and rural location being important factors. The fact that the factor analysis so clearly distinguishes them from other items itself shows that absence of these housing items is not highly correlated with other aspects of deprivation.

To focus on current basic exclusion due to lack of resources, we concentrate on the basic deprivation items, but also take income into account.

Some households lack basic items – and say this is due to lack of money – but are in the middle or upper parts of the income distribution. The factors underlying this pattern have been explored using the 1987 data, within a more general framework for analysis of the relationship between such indicators of life-style/deprivation, income, and wider measures of resources, in Nolan and Whelan (1996). The case is made there that indicators of both resources and way of life can usefully be combined in measuring deprivation/poverty. We therefore look at households which are both below relative income lines *and* experiencing deprivation of one or more of what have been identified as basic deprivation indicators. Only about half the sample households falling below the relative income lines are in fact seen to be experiencing basic deprivation.

Table 5.9:

Households in poverty by labour force status of head, Ireland 1994

Labour force status	1987		1994	
	Below 50% income line	Below 60% income line and experiencing basic deprivation	Below 50% income line	Below 60% income line and experiencing basic deprivation
Employee	8.2	11.7	6.2	7.4
Self-employed	4.8	12.4	6.7	2.2
Farmer	23.7	2.1	8.9	2.8
Unemployed	37.4	36.5	32.6	35.7
Ill/Disabled	11.1	16.6	9.5	10.1
Retired	8.1	5.6	10.5	13.0
Home Duties	6.7	15.0	25.5	28.6
All	100.0	100.0	100.0	100.0

What we are primarily interested in here is whether this affects our assessment of the position of households where the head is an employee or the earnings of other members are important. Table 5.9 compares the composition of those below the 50% relative income line with the similarly-sized group below 60% and experiencing primary deprivation, in terms of labour force status of the household head. We see that in 1987 the composition of the two groups was indeed rather different. In particular, farm households made up a considerably smaller proportion of those experiencing deprivation and below the 60% line than of those below the lower income line alone. The groups which are now a more substantial proportion of 'the poor', though, are mainly households headed by someone who is ill or in home duties. Households headed by an employee increase relatively little in importance, accounting for only about 12% of households meeting the joint income/deprivation criteria. In 1994 the differences between the two groups are less, and households headed by an employee comprise only 7% of those meeting the joint income/deprivation criteria. Broadening the focus beyond the household head again does not greatly increase the importance of earnings for poor households: in 1994, only 15% of households below the 60% income line and experiencing basic deprivation contain an employee, and in 1987 the figure was 18%. Whether current income or income plus deprivation is used, then, the 'working poor' receiving or relying on income from employment constitute at most only about 15% of 'the poor' in the Irish case.

6 POVERTY AND LOW PAY

We now turn from the role of earnings in the incomes of poor/low income households to the relationship between low pay and poverty. Low pay is conventionally measured in terms of the gross earnings of the individual, and related to benchmarks derived from the distribution of earnings. Poverty status, on the other hand, is usually assessed on the basis of the disposable equivalent income of the household, and the relationship between the two is by no means straightforward. Applying the OECD low pay cut-off to the individual earners in the 1994 Irish sample, we found that about 24% of full-time employees are below two-thirds of median gross weekly earnings. If these are taken for the purpose of the exercise to be the 'low paid', to what extent do low pay and household poverty overlap?

Table 5.10 shows that, using the relative income poverty lines, the degree of overlap is quite limited both in 1987 and 1994. In 1987, only 9% of low-paid employees were in households below half average income, 19% were in households below the 60% line, and 10% were in households below that line and experiencing basic deprivation. In 1994, the corresponding figures are a good deal lower, at 6%, 13% and 6% respectively. This is primarily because, as we have seen, most of the households below the income lines do not contain an employee, whether low paid or otherwise. From a household perspective, then, in 1994 15% of households below the 60% income line contained an employee, only 6% contain a (full-time) low-paid employee. Analysis for 1987 showed that this pattern is not altered by using the family/tax unit rather than the household as recipient unit in measuring poverty. Nor is it significantly altered by using poverty gaps or shortfalls rather than simple headcounts. The average poverty gap for poor households containing a low-paid individual is greater than the average gap for all poor households, but this only means for example that such households account for about 7% of the total poverty gap with the 60% relative income line.

Table 5.10:

The overlap between low pay and household poverty, Ireland

	1987	1994
A: % of low-paid individuals in poor households:		
Household below 50% of mean income	8.9	5.5
Household below 60% of mean income	19.5	13.3
Household below 60% of mean income + experiencing basic deprivation	10.3	6.4
B: % of poor households containing a low-paid individual		
Household below 50% of mean income	7.0	4.3
Household below 60% of mean income	9.3	5.5
Household below 60% of mean income + experiencing basic deprivation	8.6	6.3

Note: Full-time employees only, weekly low-pay threshold 2/3 of median gross earnings.

Most low-paid employees are not in 'poor' households for two main reasons. The first is that the (take-home pay corresponding to the gross) low-pay threshold is substantially higher than the relative poverty lines for a single adult or a couple, so such a household may not be below the lines even if relying entirely on the earnings of the low-paid individual. In 1994, for example, the two-thirds of median earnings threshold is IR£165 per week gross, which for a single person corresponds to about £126 net, whereas even the 60% relative income line is only about £80 for a single person. The second is that many households containing a low-paid individual are *not* depending on his/her earnings as the main income source. Many of the low paid are young adults living in the parental home or married women, and the household generally has other earners or is in receipt of social welfare transfers. A limited overlap between low pay and poverty is thus a common finding in UK and US studies. For example, Layard, Piachaud and Stewart (1978) and Bazen (1988) found that between 10–22% of low-paid workers were in families below conventionally-used poverty lines in the UK, while Burkhauser and Finnegan (1989) reported about 8–18% for the USA. The precise extent of the overlap depends on the way in which low pay and poverty are measured (which differs across these studies), but the broad message is consistent with our findings for Ireland.

Low pay does affect a significant proportion of that relatively small set of poor households which contain an employee. Depending on the poverty line and the low-pay threshold chosen, between one-third and a half of all the poor households which do contain an employee contain a low-paid employee. Thus while any policy aimed at the working poor will (directly) benefit only a minority of poor households, increased take-home pay for those below low-pay thresholds would help a substantial proportion of the working poor – though most of those benefiting will not be in poor households. What distinguishes the minority of low-paid employees who are in poor households is *not* that they have lower earnings than the majority of low-paid employees. Rather, it is the fact that the household is largely dependent on their earnings, and the fact that most of these households contain children. This has important implications for the likely immediate impact which even a minimum wage which left employment levels unaffected would have on household poverty. Ireland does not at present have a national minimum wage, with a limited number of sectoral or occupational wage minima set by Joint Labour Committees, very much on the model of the old UK Wages Councils. However, the Government which took office in Ireland in the summer of 1997 is committed to the introduction of an hourly national minimum wage, and has set up a National Minimum Wage Commission to advise on how best to do so. As elsewhere, much of the debate has focused on the impact this might have on employment, but the direct impact one would expect a minimum wage on its own to have on household poverty is in any case limited given the relationship between low pay and poverty documented here. (This has been explored for the UK in Johnson and Stark (1991) and Sutherland (1991) and for Ireland in Callan and Nolan (1992) and Nolan (1993).

This in turn focuses attention on the broader range of policies to help families with children, which can have a more immediate impact on poverty both among those depending on earnings and those on social welfare. Such static analyses clearly only provide part of the story, however. The consequences of long-term low pay interspersed with periods of unemployment are clearly much more serious than those of low pay experienced for a relatively short period, perhaps at an early stage in the working career. This points to the need for dynamic analyses of earnings mobility, which are increasingly becoming possible as suitable panel data become more widely available (see for example Atkinson, Bourguignon and Morrison, 1992, Gittleman and Joyce, 1995, OECD, 1996). In the Irish case, the panel data from the Irish element of the European Community Household Panel now coming on stream opens up the prospect of such dynamic analysis of earnings mobility and the relationship between low pay and poverty.

7   CONCLUSIONS

The earnings distribution in Ireland exhibits wider dispersion in 1994 than it did in 1987. This increase in dispersion was pronounced at the top of the distribution, and is seen for hourly earnings among all employees and weekly earnings among all full-time employees, and also for men only. Using the OECD benchmark of two-thirds of median weekly earnings, 24% of full-time employees were low paid in 1994, up from 21% in 1987 and higher than the (roughly) corresponding figures for most of the 15 countries covered in the recent OECD analysis of the extent of low pay.

Only a small minority of these low-paid employees were in poor households in 1987 or 1994, and only a small minority of poor households contain a low-paid employee. These conclusions hold whether household poverty is measured using relative income poverty lines, or using a combination of income and non-monetary indicators of deprivation. The dynamics of low pay and poverty need to be understood before one can draw firm conclusions about the relationship between low pay and household poverty and its implications.

NOTES

1   See Bradley *et al.* (1997) for an in-depth assessment of the recent Irish growth experience.
2   See for example Teague (1995), O'Donnell and O'Reardon (1996).
3   OECD (1996) Table P6t, p. 130, Table P3, p. 122.
4   Earnings functions estimated with this dataset have been presented in Callan (1991) for married men and married women, Nolan (1993) for the entire sample, and Callan and Wren (1994) for men and women and for married versus single men and women.
5   Such relative income cut-offs also constitute one element of the official UK series on Households Below Average Income produced by the Department of Social Security (DSS) (e.g. DSS 1996).
6   The corresponding figures for 1987 were slightly higher, at 14% and 20% respectively.
7   In fact, the year covered by our 1987 survey was a particularly bad year for income from farming in Ireland.

REFERENCES

Atkinson, A.B. (1985), *How Should We Measure Poverty?*, ESRC Programme on Taxation, Incentives and the Distribution of Income, Discussion Paper No. 82, London School of Economics.

Atkinson, A.B. (1987), 'On The Measurement of Poverty', *Econometrica*, **5**, 749–764.

Atkinson, A.B., F. Bourguignon and C. Morrison, (1992), *Empirical Studies of Earnings Mobility*, Harwood.

Bazen, S. (1988), *On the Overlap Between Low Pay and Poverty*, ESRC Programme on Taxation, Incentives and the Distribution of Income, Discussion Paper No. 120, London School of Economics.

Bradley, J., J. FitzGerald, P. Honohan, and I. Kearney (1997), 'Interpreting the Recent Irish Growth Experience', in Duffy, D., J. FitzGerald, I. Kearney, and F. Shortall, (eds.), *Medium-Term Review: 1997–2003*, Dublin: The Economic and Social Research Institute.

Buhman, B., L. Rainwater, G. Schmaus and T. Smeeding (1988), 'Equivalence Scales, Well-being, Inequality and Poverty: Sensitivity Estimates Across Ten Countries using the Luxembourg Income Study Database', *Review of Income and Wealth*, **33**, 115–142.

Burkhauser, R. and T. Finnegan (1989). 'The Minimum Wage and the Poor: The End of the Relationship', *Journal of Policy Analysis and Management*, **8**, 53–71.

Callan, T. (1991), 'Male-Female Wage Differentials in Ireland', *Economic and Social Review*, **23**, 55–72.

Callan, T. and B. Nolan (1991), 'Concepts of Poverty and the Poverty Line', *Journal of Economic Surveys*, **5**, 243–261.

Callan, T. and B. Nolan (1992). 'Concepts of Poverty and the Poverty Line: A Critical Survey of Approaches to Measuring Poverty', *Journal of Economic Surveys*, 5, (3), 243–62.

Callan, T. and A. Wren (1994), *Male-Female Wage Differentials: Analysis and Policy Issues*, General Research Series Paper No. 163, Dublin: The Economic and Social Research Institute.

Callan, T., B. Nolan and C.T. Whelan (1993), 'Resources, Deprivation and the Measurement of Poverty', *Journal of Social Policy*, **22**, 141–72.

Callan, T., B. Nolan *et al.*, (1989), *Poverty, Income and Welfare in Ireland*, General Research Series No. 146, Dublin: The Economic and Social Research Institute.

Callan, T., B. Nolan, B.J. Whelan, C.T. Whelan and J. Williams, (1996), *Poverty in the 1990s: Evidence from the 1994 Living in Ireland Survey*, General Research Series No. 146, Dublin: Oaktree Press.

Cantillon, S. and B. Nolan (1998), 'Are Married Women More Deprived than their Husbands?', *Journal of Social Policy*, vol (2), 151–71.

Centre d'Etudes des Revenus et des Couts (1991), *Les Bas Salaires dans les Pays de la Communauté Economique Européenne*, Paris: CERC.

Coulter, F., F. Cowell and S. Jenkins (1992), 'Equivalence Scale Relativities and the Extent of Poverty and Inequality', *Economic Journal*, **102**, 1067–82.

Department of Social Security (1996), *Households Below Average Income: A Statistical Analysis 1979–1993/94*, London: Government Statistical

Service.

Fahey, T. and J. FitzGerald, (1997), 'The Educational Revolution and Demographic Change', in Duffy, D., J. FitzGerald, I. Kearney, and F. Shortall, (eds.), *Medium-Term Review: 1997-2003*, Dublin: The Economic and Social Research Institute.

Forster, M. (1994), *Measurement of Low Incomes and Poverty in a Perspective of International Comparisons,* Labour Market and Social Policy Occasional Papers, No. 14, Paris: OECD.

Foster, J. and A.F. Shorrocks (1988), 'Poverty Orderings', *Econometrica*, **56**, 173–177.

Gittleman, M. and M. Joyce, (1995), 'Earnings Mobility in the United States, 1967-91', *Monthly Labour Review*, September, 3–13.

Hagenaars, A., K. de Vos, and M. A. Zaidi, (1994), *Patterns of Poverty in Europe*, paper presented to Seminar on the Measurement and Analysis of Social Exclusion, Commission of the European Communities/Department of Social Security, Bath: Centre for Research in European Social and Employment Policy.

Harmon, C. and I. Walker (1995), 'Estimates of the Economic Return to Schooling for the United Kingdom', *American Economic Review*, **85**, 1278–1286.

Hughes, G., and B. Nolan (1996), 'Pension Plans and Labor Market Structure: Evidence from Ireland', in E. Reynaud, L. apRoberts, B. Davies, and G. Hughes with the collaboration of T. Ghilarducci and J. Turner, (eds), *International Perspectives on Supplementary Pensions: Actors and Issues.* Westport CT: Quorum Books.

ISSAS (Institute of Social Studies Advisory Service) (1990) *Poverty in Figures: Europe in the Early 1980s,* Luxembourg: Eurostat.

Johnson, P. and G. Stark (1991), 'The Effects of a Minimum Wage on Family Incomes', *Fiscal Studies*, **12**, 88–93.

Layard, R., D. Piachaud and M. Stewart (1978), *The Causes of Poverty*, Background Paper No. 5, Royal Commission on the Distribution of Income and Wealth, London: HMSO.

Mack, J. and S. Lansley (1985), *Poor Britain*, London: Allen and Unwin.

Muffels, R. (1993) 'Deprivation standards and style of living indices', in Berghman, J. and Cantillon, B. (1993), *The European Face of Social Security*, Aldershot: Avebury.

Nickell, S. and C. Bean (1996), 'Changes in the Distribution of Wages and Unemployment in OECD Countries', *American Economic Review*, May,

Nolan, B. (1993), *Low Pay in Ireland*, General Research Series Paper No. 159, Dublin: The Economic and Social Research Institute.

Nolan, B. and T. Callan, eds., (1994), *Poverty and Policy in Ireland*, Dublin: Gill and Macmillan.

Nolan, B. and C.T. Whelan (1996), *Resources, Deprivation and Poverty*, Oxford: Clarendon Press.

O'Donnell, R. and O'Reardon, C. (1996), 'The Irish Experiment', *New Economy*, **3**, 33–38.

OECD (1993), *Employment Outlook*, Paris: OECD.

OECD (1996), *Employment Outlook*, Paris: OECD.

O'Higgins, M. and S. Jenkins (1989), 'Poverty in the EC: Estimates for 1975, 1980 and 1985', in R. Teekens and B.M.S. van Praag (eds): *Analysing Poverty in the European Community*, Eurostat News Special Edition 1 – 1990, Luxembourg.

Sexton, J. and P. O'Connell, (eds), (1997), *Labour Market Studies: Ireland*, Luxembourg: Office for Official Publications of the European Communities.

Sutherland, H. (1991), *The Immediate Impact of a Minimum Wage on Family Incomes*, Microsimulation Modelling Unit Research Note 1, STICERD, London School of Economics, London.

Teague, P. (1995), 'Pay Determination in the Republic of Ireland: Towards Social Corporatism?', *British Journal of Industrial Relations*, **33**, 253–73.

Townsend, P. (1979), *Poverty in the United Kingdom*, Harmondsworth: Penguin.

6. Atypical Work as a Form of Low-Wage Employment in the German Labour Market

Holger Buch and Peter Rühmann

---

1 INTRODUCTION

Due to the institutional framework, low-wage employment in the sense of 'working poor' is almost neglible in the conventional German labour market; however, there has been an ever-increasing call of late for the development of low-wage employment. The protagonists propose this as a solution to the employment crisis of the past two decades, especially in connection with job opportunities for the unskilled. As support for their case they cite the increase in employment in the US-labour market, where a large portion of the new jobs are low paid. There are, however, presently two atypical forms of employment in Germany which could be identified as a form of low-wage employment in a broader sense. For these the usual institutional arrangements are not valid.

This chapter begins by presenting the institutional framework that prevents the emergence of low-wage employment within the conventional German labour market. After that, the two types of atypical employment relationships with a marginally low payment (especially in consideration of indirect components, for example social security benefits, holiday with pay etc.) are described. As a further step, problems resulting from this development are analysed. Finally, some possible policy measures are discussed.

2 THE INSTITUTIONAL FRAMEWORK IN THE CONVENTIONAL LABOUR MARKET

In the conventional labour market of Germany (i.e. the supply and the demand of employment which is obligatorily integrated into the social security system), low-wage employment[1] comparable to the US could not develop. The continuing absence of a legal minimum wage depends upon two decisive factors: collective agreements and social transfers.

Firstly, collective wage agreements fix the wage category and the level of earnings for about 90% of all wage and salary earners. Despite the fact that only 39% of the employees are unionized, generally all employees of an employer who is bound by a collective agreement receive the same wage; no matter whether they are union members or not. In addition, many employers who are not formally bound by a collective wage agreement also apply its regulations. As a consequence, centralized wage negotiations between unions and employers' associations determine the lowest wage level for most employment relationships.

Secondly, the wages at the lowest level are also influenced by social transfers in cases of unemployment (i.e. unemployment benefits, unemployment relief and social assistance). Taking into account the need for an incentive to resume employment, there must be an adequate difference between earnings from work and social transfers. Hence, the so-called social safety net also contributes to the setting of a minimum level of wages, that is significantly higher than social transfers.

Figure 6.1:
Minimum wage in the German labour market

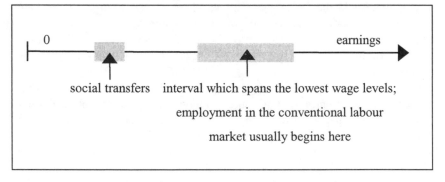

Consequently, a minimum wage exists, although it is not possible to fix its exact amount. Furthermore, it differs somewhat from branch to branch. As a consequence, an interval spanning the lowest wage levels of all branches can be identified (Figure 6.1). Although there is no official minimum wage in Germany *de jure*, there is one *de facto*. A minimum level, however, is not a sufficient means to prevent the existence of low-paid jobs. Considering the US labour market as an example, the legal minimum wage has not prevented the emergence of the 'working poor'. Therefore it is necessary to set the minimum wage at a sufficiently high level. In Germany this level is mainly influenced by union bargaining power in collective negotiations and the level of social transfers. The unions' maxim is twofold. Firstly, they try to achieve an income sufficiently high to form the basis of existence for a family. Secondly, they try to enforce more than proportional wage increases for the lower wage groups.[2] Social transfers, the other significant factor for the level of the lowest wages, should at least secure the minimum standard of subsistence.

In contrast to the US, this framework prevents the emergence of low-wage employment in the conventional German labour market.[3] Nevertheless, many participants in the discussion about mass unemployment in Germany support forms of low-wage employment as a means of creating new jobs.[4] In fact, outside the conventional labour market forms of employment which could be characterized as low-wage employment in a broader sense do already exist. These are the so-called 'geringfügige Beschäftigung', and 'dependent self-employment'[5]. Both belong to the atypical forms of employment[6], which will be identified in the following section.

3 ATYPICAL FORMS OF EMPLOYMENT PERMITTING THE PAYMENT OF LOW WAGES

Atypical work is a collective term for forms of employment differing from a standard employment relationship, that is classified as an unlimited full-time job with the usual labour and social rights. Atypical work includes temporary work, fixed-term contracts, part-time work, 'geringfügige Beschäftigung' and dependent self-employment.

Recently, the quantitative importance of atypical employment has increased drastically. As Figure 6.2 shows, more than one third of all employment relationships now belong to the atypical work category. The main reason for this development is due to the rise in 'geringfügiger Beschäftigung' and dependent self-employment. Due to their exclusion from the social security system, both forms are also described by the term unprotected employment relationships. Thus, they do not belong to the conventional labour market unlike the other three forms of atypical work, which, although they are not standard employment relationships, are included in the social security system and the institutional framework described above is applicable to them.

In 1995 there were nearly seven million unprotected employment relationships. These jobs could be classified as low-wage employment in a broader sense because they allow the employer to pay a wage lower than the quasi minimum wage as described earlier. In a broader sense this means that not only the gross earnings have to be considered; the costs accessory to wages are also components of earnings and represent a part of total labour costs.

Figure 6.2

Development of unprotected employment relationships ('geringfügige Beschäftigung' plus dependent self-employment), atypical work and standard jobs in Western Germany, 1975–95

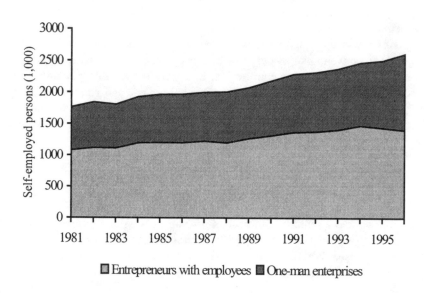

■ Entrepreneurs with employees ■ One-man enterprises

The 'geringfügige Beschäftigung'

In Germany, wage and salary earners are automatically members of the social security system[7] which consists of health-, nursing-, unemployment- and pension-insurance. The 'geringfügige Beschäftigung' is the exception. This special type of part-time work is excluded from the social security system. Figure 6.3 shows the conditions of such an employment relationship, which are mainly contingent upon the two factors of hours worked and income.

In 1996 there were 6.7 million of these jobs in Germany – about 3.9 million in business and 2.8 million in private households. About 4 million people were exclusively working as 'geringfügig Beschäftigte', an additional 1.4 million had a corresponding secondary job. Thus, some people have more than one of these jobs.[8] From 1991 to 1996 the number of these employment relationships has risen by more than 37%. In the same period the number of jobs in the conventional labour market has more or less stagnated in the face of rising unemployment. Consequently, it is justified to speak of a real boom in supplementary employment.

Most of these jobs are unskilled or semi-skilled. As mentioned above, private households have a great demand for these jobs. Moreover, they are mainly found in the service sector, especially in the distributive trade, in cleaning and in the hotel and restaurant business. People working in 'geringfügiger Beschäftigung' are a very heterogeneous group. Married housewives (47%), students (13%), school pupils (12%), pensioners (10%) and the unemployed (7%)[9] are typical for those who have no other job.[10] If it is a secondary job, one can assume that the workers have a main occupation and are thereby subject to social security contributions. Women typically use the option of 'geringfügige Beschäftigung': three quarters of the persons who are exclusively employed in this way are female.

Figure 6.3

Definition of 'geringfügige Beschäftigung'

= form of employment that is excluded from the social security system

(3 variants)

	1) Low income	2) Short-term employment	3) Special terms
Hours worked	Hours/week less than 15	Employment is restricted to 2 months or 50 working days during the year	For students and pensioners
Income	i) Less than DM 620 per month or ii) Less than 1/6 of the total income per year, 'secondary job'	Not professionally working, i.e. not a main income	

The engagement of 'geringfügig Beschäftigte' offers the employer a higher degree of flexibility because labour demand can easily be brought into line with the actual requirements. What is more, costs can be reduced to a significant degree. To make a comparison Figure 6.4 shows the costs of socially secured employment (i.e. in the conventional labour market) per hour. The costs accessory to wages amount to 46% of the total labour costs. In other words, the gross hourly wages must nearly be doubled to get the total labour costs. In case of 'geringfügiger Beschäftigung' the employers save the social security contribution, which amounts to more than 20% of the gross earnings. If the employer is bound by a collective agreement, he has to apply these agreements also to the 'geringfügig Beschäftigten'.

Figure 6.4
Labour costs and earnings in the case of employment integrated
in the social security system

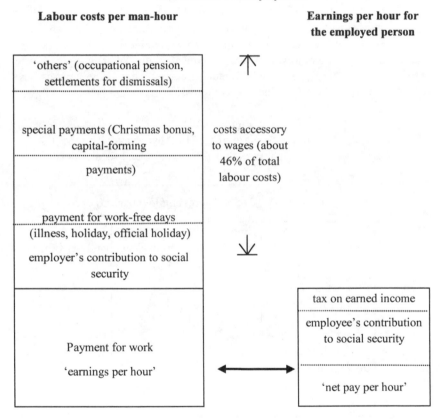

Nevertheless, it is safe to assume that these people get lower wages. A recent investigation shows that the gross wages per hour are 14% lower than for part-time work that is subject to social security contributions.[11] Moreover, although after a certain period of employment, industrial and social laws become applicable for these jobs, they are often disregarded. In general, the employees accept these conditions because they are not informed adequately of their rights or are afraid of losing their job. Both aspects are reinforced by the low level of unionization. Therefore, there is a wide potential for reducing labour costs[12] even when the same wages per hour are paid. Thus, at least from the employers' point of view one can speak of the existence of low-wage employment.

An example will serve to illustrate this. The average wage per hour of a student-worker in the catering trade in Göttingen amounts to approximately DM 13. This wage represents the total labour costs for the employer as well as the gross = net wage for the student. The corresponding standard hourly wage is DM 13.89; i.e. the total labour costs amount to approximately DM 26 per hour (including costs accessory to wages, see Figure 6.4). Thus, 'geringfügige Beschäftigung' leads to cost reduction of about a half.

In general, this kind of low-wage employment is not leading to a financially precarious situation for the employed person. For them gainful employment has nearly always a supplementary character (students, pupils, pensioners etc.). Others have additional earnings from their first job. The net earnings can attain an attractive level, even if the wage is lower than the standard wage: the employees do not have to pay the 20% social security contribution. Besides, in many cases there is no wage tax because of low income or the employer uses the option of a lump sum taxation. Thereby it is even possible that the net hourly earnings per hour are higher than in the conventional labour market. This might seem a paradox, since the 'geringfügige Beschäftigung' was identified above as a form of low-wage employment. However, the amount of the total labour costs justify this classification.

Dependent Self-Employment

These persons attain the status of 'self-employed' in name only; considering the actual circumstances they remain employees. They are strongly bound by the instructions of their principal and they have hardly any freedom to make their own management decisions. Some typical characteristics are: they generally receive their tasks from only one 'customer' (i.e. principal); they are strongly integrated in the principal's organization; they have no employees (one-man-enterprise); they have no ability to set the price; their working time is determined and the capitalization is very low or completely missing.

Industrial and social laws have to be applied to employees but not to the self-employed. This requires a dividing line between 'employee' and 'self-employed'. In reality, a clear distinction is not always possible because there is no legal definition. The degree of dependence is decisive for the status. However, in many cases this degree is very difficult to determine for an observer on the outside. The contracting parties benefit from these circumstances. They can declare salaried employment as self-employment, though this is an illegal act. The employer then has the possibility to convert a standard employment relationship into this form of atypical work. To make this point clear; it is illegal to negotiate about the status; however, since both contracting parties share a common interest, these cases often remain undiscovered.

Figure 6.5
Self-employed persons outside the primary sector
1981–1996, Western Germany

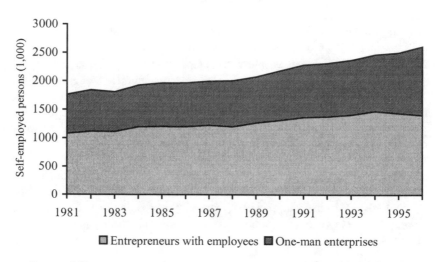

□ Entrepreneurs with employees ■ One-man enterprises

Source: Mikrozensus

The problem described above of identification makes it impossible to find out the exact extent of dependent self-employment. Having said that dependent self-employed persons have no employees, the number of one-man enterprises could be a first clue[13] (Figure 6.5). In Western Germany, between 1981 and 1996 this number has risen by 77%. In the same period the number of entrepreneurs with employees has risen by only 30%.[14] Meanwhile nearly half of all 2.6 million self-employed persons have no employees. One reason for this development can be found in the rise of dependent self-employment.

A recent study estimates the number of dependent self-employed persons at between 400,000 and more than 1 million, depending on the chosen method.[15] There are two arguments for a further increase in this form of unprotected employment relationship; firstly, the expected increase in the costs accessory to wages makes it more attractive. Secondly, more and more trades/occupations are beginning to realize the possibilities and 'advantages' of dependent self-employment. Typical examples for this kind of work are: insurance company representatives, truck drivers in the transport trade, construction workers, shop assistants, freelancers who work in the media but also white-collar workers whose contracts of employment were replaced by consultancy agreements.

From the employer's point of view there are several advantages in hiring a dependent self-employed person: the labour costs can be reduced because the employer is bound neither by a collective agreement nor by industrial and social laws, and what is particularly important, no social security contributions are payable in the case of self-employment. All settlements, especially payments, are subject to negotiations between the contracting parties. As a result of these negotiations, a reduction in the total labour costs is only to be expected. Generally, employers have a stronger position in individual wage negotiations than the employees. This is especially true in times of mass unemployment. If the employer could not achieve a reduction of the total labour costs there would be hardly any incentive for him to prefer such an employment relationship to a standard one.

Another advantage for the employer is the greater degree of flexibility. There is a direct connection between labour demand and output, which means that the factor labour loses its quasi-fixed character.[16] There are far-reaching consequences for the German economy. Despite the fact that there is a relatively extensive protection against dismissals, an American-style 'hire and fire' policy becomes possible for the firms involved.

Finally, the engagement of dependent self-employed persons is also advantageous to the employers because these persons obviously have no right to participate in the firm's decision-making process. From the dependent self-employed person's point of view, the situation is different. If he wants to achieve an income equivalent to that of a standard employed individual, all the components of Figure 6.4 must be considered. Taking into account the loss of the benefits of accessory wage components, the hourly wage for the self-employed person must nearly be doubled. Moreover, he should get compensation for the risk he has to carry. As stated above, it must be assumed that the total income of a dependent self-employed person will be considerably lower, because he has to forego several benefits (for example, no paid holidays, discontinuation of wage payment during periods of sickness etc.).

As part of the study of precarious financial situations, several field studies support this thesis.[17] In a recent study, the following data about the income of dependent self-employed persons were published: gross median earnings of principal occupations amount to approximately DM 2800 compared to median earnings of DM 4000 a month (annual bonus not included) in 1994.[18] Even if one has to be careful with these numbers, they confirm the thesis identifying dependent self-employment as a form of low-wage employment in the German labour market.

What remains to be considered is why employees are willing to sign such a contract. There are three main reasons. The first is the lack of an alternative in the conventional labour market. In other words, the high level of unemployment is a necessary precondition for the observed development.[19] Secondly, the people concerned are usually unable to compare in a realistic way their incomes to those of others. This is due to the fact that they are unable to value correctly the industrial and social benefits. The income of self-employed persons might seem quite attractive at first sight, because the employee's social security contributions are left out.[20] Finally the wage tax does not directly reduce the income in the case of self-employment (no collection of tax at source). As a consequence, these people fail to see the facts of their financial situation (money illusion). This is reinforced by the common view that the move to self-employment is a form of social advancement.

Furthermore, one should keep in mind that the future of the pension insurance based on a pay-as-you-go system is discussed critically in the public. Demographic developments (i.e. decline of birth rates) will lead to declining benefit rates.[21] This might lead to a lower valuation of the expected benefits. In the extreme case these contributions (which after all amount to one fifth of the gross wage) are not considered as a component of income and therefore are not considered in the comparison of incomes either.

These explanations show that both forms of atypical work have to be identified as low-wage employment. Earnings and respectively total labour costs are considerably lower than in the conventional labour market.

4   CONSEQUENCES

The recently observed increase in unprotected employment relationships has numerous consequences. In that this is a relatively new process, a full evaluation cannot be undertaken, however a number of effects at different levels can be described.

The Affected Population

The majority of the 'geringfügig Beschäftigten' seem to be satisfied with their situation; results of a survey suggests that only 9% are looking for another job. As shown above, it can be expected that most of the 'geringfügig Beschäftigten' are not in a precarious income situation because the earnings have a supplementary character for them. The same can be said for those persons who have similar secondary jobs, supporting their main income. In most cases, the reduction in social security contributions is also in accordance with their preferences; the missing contributions lead to an attractive net wage and are important factors for taking on such a job. The threat of a later gap in social protection is not that strong in that few workers remain involved in this type of occupation in the long term. Furthermore it is predominantly women who are concerned. Since this kind of employment does not lead to any direct claims on benefits, in this respect their situation is not different from those women who are not in gainful employment.[22]

In contrast, dependent self-employed persons face a completely different situation; their income level is frequently insufficient. In the short- and medium-term this can be compensated by longer hours and renunciation of holiday; thereby, a direct social decline can be avoided. Weightier consequences should be expected due to insufficient social security, particularly in provisions for old age. The reasons are small incomes combined with lack of foresight. In addition, there could be a problem of moral hazard. If their provisions are insufficient, the dependent self-employed persons can still count on social assistance. In short, such an employment relationship leads to an accumulation of bad risks without suitable compensation for the employee. The severity of this development remains difficult to estimate (for example when compared to the American phenomenon of the 'working poor'). The actual supply of data does not allow a concrete evaluation.

Firms: Employers and Competitors

An employer using unprotected employment relationships can achieve a competitive advantage. This is mainly due to the reduction of costs (see the sections above on 'geringfügige Beschäftigung' and Dependent Self Employment). In other words, competitors not using unprotected relationships are in a less competitive position. This is strengthened by the fact that the increasing social security contributions (see below) following the conversion leads to a rise in labour costs, too. This is crucial in the case of dependent self-employment, because the competitive advantage is caused by an illegal form of employment relationship and can thus be construed as a form of unfair competition. Possibly, more and more employers have to convert jobs from the conventional labour market in order to restore their competitive ability. Consequently, an erosion of employment relationships that are subject to social security contributions might be expected.

Total Employment

The increase in unprotected employment relationships has to be seen in connection with the development of jobs that are subject to social security contributions. The conversion of jobs from the conventional labour market is a major factor in the expansion of these atypical forms of work. Employers are especially interested in these atypical forms of work, regarding it is as an opportunity to reduce costs. They split a full-time job into several 'geringfügige Beschäftigungen' or they charge self-employed persons with doing the work.

The increase in 'geringfügiger Beschäftigung' itself is a proof of such a substitution. In the last decade the number of people exclusively working as 'geringfügig Beschäftigte' in Western Germany has nearly doubled. This drastic rise cannot be explained by structural change and its effects on labour demand. In the past, this labour demand was effective in the conventional labour market. Also, by far the greatest part of the dependent self-employed activities are jobs which were formerly integrated in the social security system. Sometimes those who are affected are former employees to whom a further contractual occupation is offered if they accept the status of being self-employed.[23]

Total employment remains untouched by this substitution process. It is only those occupations, demanded solely due to the lower costs, which lead to a higher level of employment. The non-existence of low-paid jobs in the conventional labour market can explain some of the unprotected employment relationships (especially 'geringfügige Beschäftigung'). Due to low productivity, these jobs are not profitable in the conventional labour market. Simply speaking, without forms of atypical work these jobs would no longer exist.[24] The same, however, cannot be said for the dependent self-employment because in most cases it has a complementary character. This means that the work is a necessary component of the entire production process. Moreover, most of the activities can be found in branches where international competition is less strong. Therefore, it seems justified to argue that the growth of dependent self-employment is almost exclusively a conversion of jobs from the conventional labour market. For the 'geringfügige Beschäftigung' the same can at least be said with regard to the greatest part of the recently established jobs.

Consequences for the Exchequer

The employer has different options in regard to the taxation of incomes resulting from 'geringfügiger Beschäftigung'. Consequently, a loss of revenue results in the change of social secured work into these jobs when the cheaper alternative is chosen. Besides, the scope for tax evasion increases if jobs are converted into self-employment: in the case of wage earning employment there is a collection of tax at source, therefore there is hardly any possibility of evading taxes. Things are quite different in the case of self-employed persons because they have to file a tax return. Therefore, it can happen that the tax office is not informed correctly about the taxable income. In addition, there is the danger of increasing government expenditures, as the state must pay social benefits in the event of missing claims on benefits from the social security system.

The Social Security System

Certain institutional arrangements within the social security system necessitate increased contributions when social secured employment relationships are converted into unprotected ones.[25] A main reason is that the financial basis of the pension insurance dwindles, the sum of incomes that is subject to contributions declines and there is a loss of revenues. On the other hand, reduced claims on social security benefits will only ease the system's burden with a time lag (pay-as-you-go system). In the meantime the system will get into financial difficulties which can only be compensated by higher contributions.

As far as health insurance is concerned, contributions will also rise. This is due to the fact that most of the 'geringfügig Beschäftigten' have indirect insurance cover (e.g. husbands, students etc.). They do not have to pay contributions even though they have an income. This can be seen as a kind of free-rider behaviour. Therefore, labour costs in the conventional labour market will rise in conjunction with declining employment opportunities.

5   REFORMS

The previous examples point to undesirable consequences which indicate necessary economic policy measures. The main problem of the 'geringfügige Beschäftigung' may be seen as a 'legal' misuse if former social secured jobs are converted into this kind of employment. This contradicts the original idea driving the legislation, which was to provide this kind of employment in response to a labour demand of limited size. The aim should not be to abolish the 'geringfügige Beschäftigung' generally, only the legal abuse thereof. Therefore, changes within the institutional framework should be given precedence. A first step could be a higher and obligatory lump-sum taxation of the incomes in order to make the user responsible for self initiated costs (free-rider behaviour in the social security system). Employers would still be in a flexible position. On the other hand, the quasi-subsidization of these jobs would be eliminated. As secondary jobs are those mainly concerned, making them subject to social security contributions seems to be a sensible solution. It is a paradox that overtime payment in a standard employment relationship is subject to social security contributions, whereas the same person can have a secondary job without having to pay contributions.

In contrast, in the case of dependent self-employment, its very existence is contrary to the original legislation in that protection is deemed necessary in dependent occupations. A promising solution could be to reduce the incentive to use dependent self-employment. Therefore, a first step could be to make these forms of employment subject to social security contributions. The mandatory integration in the social security system would result in the dependent self-employed individuals' awareness of the costs of social security protection. Increased 'wage' demands would lead to a decreased incentive to hire such a person. In practice, however, the problem remains to distinguish a dependent self-employed person from the entire population of independent businessmen. One approach could be to restrict the measure to those who have no employees (identified above as one clue for dependent self-employment).

In general it remains to be questioned whether the actual practice in Germany is sensible in taking status as the indicator for the need of protection. For example, a self-employed taxi driver with a monthly income of DM 1500 is not automatically integrated in the social security system whereas a top manager in the status of a salary earner is a compulsory member. The income level would probably be a better indicator.

6   SUMMARY

The institutional framework prevents the development of low-wage employment in the conventional German labour market. However, the market has found niches which allow employment with lower labour costs. There are two forms of atypical work which are excluded from the social security system: the 'geringfügige Beschäftigung' and the dependent self-employment. These forms make low-wage employment possible in Germany, if only in a more or less indirect way. The number of these employment relationships has increased in recent years and is now estimated to have reached a level of nearly 7 million. When talking about low-wage employment in Germany, these unprotected employment relationships must be taken into account. Different approaches neglect this fact. For example, the OECD only considers the gross monthly earnings of full-time, full year workers including the proportional supplementary payments.[26] This means that the forms of atypical work discussed here are ignored completely.

The accompanying consequences may point to a need for political counter-measures. After all, the expansion of unprotected employment relationships reduces the level of employment in the conventional labour market. The erosion of incomes that are subject to social security contributions can lead to substantial problems for the social security system.

As a final conclusion it must be said that this kind of low-wage employment is definitely no way to reduce unemployment.

NOTES

1. This study considers the phenomenon of low-wage employment in a predominantly qualitative sense. It is therefore not necessary to give a concrete definition. For other approaches, see for instance OECD (1996).
2. These are also reasons for the relatively small wage spread in Germany. For example, the minimum wage in the US is 39% of the average earnings, whereas in Germany the 'pseudo minimum wage' is about 55%.
3. This, however, does not necessarily mean that in the conventional German labour market there are no workers in the lower income brackets.
4. See, for instance Berthold and Fehn (1996).
5. In Germany this is called 'Scheinselbständigkeit' or 'abhängige Selbständigkeit'. Similar forms of this dependent self-employment are known in other states. In the U.S. this is called 'independent contracting' in France 'travailleurs indépendants', in Belgium 'faux indépendants' and in the UK 'controlled self-employed'.
6. Illicit work, which can also be classified as low-wage employment, is left out of this study because it is not official employment.
7. See Buch and Rühmann (forthcoming).
8. This was called conventional labour market above.
9. Estimates of figures of 'geringfügiger Beschäftigung' vary considerably. The data mentioned here are according to Deutsches Institut für Wirtschaftsforschung (1997a).
10. Jobless persons are allowed to work less than 15 hours a week.
11. Friedrich (1993), p. 556.
12. Deutsches Institut für Wirtschaftsforschung (1997 b), p.
13. In some cases, the employer has to pay a lump sum tax of about 20% of the income – this reduces the savings a little.
14. But of course, not all of them are dependent self-employed persons.
15. The primary sector is left out because dependent self-employment is not relevant there.
16. Dietrich (1996).
17. Oi (1962).
18. Mayer and Paasch (1990).
19. OECD (1996), p. 105.
20. Generally, a positive correlation between level of unemployment and number of self-employed persons can be empirically proved.
21. The social security contributions amount to approximately 42% of gross earnings; one half is taken from the employee's gross earnings, the other half is paid by the employer.
22. The pension benefits in a pay-as-you-go system depend on the rate of population growth and income growth.
23. This problem is a consequence of the fact that only employment in the conventional labour market leads to direct claims on social security.
24. Mayer and Paasch (1990).
25. Most employment statistics do not fully include the 'geringfügige Beschäftigung'. Thus, the level of total employment is underestimated.
26. Buch (1995), pp. 148.
27. OECD (1996), p. 101.

REFERENCES

Berthold, N. and Fehn, R. (1996), The Positive Economics of Unemployment and Labor Market Inflexibility, *Kyklos*, **4**, 583–613.

Buch, H. and Rühmann, P., Quantitative und qualitative Bedeutung von Nicht-Normarbeitsverhältnissen in Deutschland, in: Kommission für Zukunftsfragen der Freistaaten Bayern und Sachsen (Hrsg.), (1998), Erwerbstätigkeit und Arbeitslosigkeit in Deutschland. Entwicklung, Ursachen und Maßnahmen; Anlageband; Gutachten im Augtrag der Kommission für Zukunftsfragen der Freistaaten Bayern und Sachsen, Band I: Entwicklung, Bewertung und Entlohnung von Erwerbsarbeit sowie Wirkungen der Globalisierung auf die Beschäftigung, Bonn, S. 7–59.

Buch, H. (1995), Steigende Sozialversicherungsbeiträge durch Zunahme von ungeschützten Beschäftigungsverhältnissen, *Sozialer Fortschritt*, **6**, 148–154.

Deutsches Institut für Wirtschaftsforschung (1997a), Erwerbsstatistik unterschätzt Beschäftigung um 2 Millionen Personen, in: *DIW-Wochenbericht*, **38**, 689–694.

Deutsches Institut für Wirtschaftsforschung (1997b), p. 895. Einführung der Sozialversicherungspflicht für 610-Mark-Jobs und Abschaffung der Pauschalbesteuerung, in: *DIW-Wochenbericht* **45**, 895–898.

Dietrich, H. (1996), Empirische Befunde zur Scheinselbständigkeit, Bundesministerium für Arbeit und Sozialordnung (Hrsg.), Forschungsbericht Nr. 262, Bonn.

Friedrich, W. (1993), Sozialversicherungsfreie Beschäftigungsverhältnisse 1987 und 1992, *WSI Mitteilungen*, 553–560.

Mayer, U., Paasch, U. (1990), Ein Schein von Selbständigkeit. Ein-Personen-Unternehmen als neue Form der Abhängigkeit, Köln.

OECD (1996), *Employment Outlook 1996*, Paris.

Oi, W.Y. (1962), Labor as a Quasi-Fixed factor, *Journal of Political Economy*, **70**, 538–555.

7.   The Effects of Minimum Wages: Evidence from Spain

Juan J. Dolado, Florentino Felgueroso and Juan F. Jimeno

1   INTRODUCTION

According to The Economist (April, 1995), 'Economists delight in making well-intentioned but hare-brained political nostrums. Minimum wage laws are a special favourite'. Since most economists in defending their faith say that by raising the cost of labour jobs will be lost, a furor has been caused by a series of recent studies which argue that minimum wages do not decrease the number of jobs – and sometimes even increase it.

The recent book by Card and Krueger (1995) and the work undertaken by Alan Manning and various co-authors on the effects of minimum wages in Europe (see, e.g. Dolado *et al.*, 1996 and Machin and Manning, 1996) assemble the revisionist evidence. In America and Europe, left-leaning politicians have greeted these results with glee. Both Democrats and the Labour Party want to reverse the whittling-down of minimum wages. For example, the real value of America's federal minimum wage has fallen by 33% since 1979 while in Britain, after the abolition of Wages Councils in 1993, only farm workers are covered. As a result, the Clinton administration proposed lifting the federal hourly minimum from $4.25 to $4.80 in 1995 and to $5.15 a year later, while the newly elected Labour government in the UK will be introducing a national minimum wage. Furthermore, the issue of establishing minimum wage is a hot one in the discussion of the Social Chapter of the future Economic and Monetary Union in Europe.

It is quite natural that the heresy is under attack. Issues related to the misuse of data, the use of appropriate control in studying the effects of minimum wage on employment, the effects on the education of teenagers who may be more likely to leave school, etc, have been raised. No doubt there is more to come from both sides. At what level do minimum wages start to cost jobs? Should they vary from industry to industry and by age? Are there tangible effects of minimum wages on the earnings distribution? These controversial questions need to be answered on the basis of empirical work. In this paper, we summarize the evidence found for Spain, a country which holds the dubious honour of having the highest unemployment rate in the OECD (20%) and, therefore, whose labour market institutions, including minimum wages, should be subject of close scrutiny.

The content of this chapter is presented in five sections. In the first section, we describe the system of minimum wages in operation in Spain, we measure its importance in terms of both the Kaitz index and the size of the spike in the wage distribution and, finally, we analyse the characteristics of the typical minimum wage earner. In sections 2, 3 and 4, we review some of the available studies and report some new evidence using alternative data sources and econometric approaches. In section 5 we draw a number of conclusions.

2   THE STATUTORY MINIMUM WAGE

The current system of statutory minimum wages in Spain, the *Salario Mínimo Interprofesional* (hereafter SMI) was established in 1964, replacing an earlier system in which fragmentary minimum wages varied by region and age. The minimum wage is set by the government in consultation with trade unions and employer organizations and its stated purpose is to protect wage earners and ensure 'a guarantee of their purchasing power and participation in the economic development of the nation' (Workers' Charter).

The SMI currently sets one rate for workers aged 18 or over and one rate for those aged 16–17 though prior to 1990 it had set different rates for 16-year-olds with special rates for houseworkers and temporary workers. Unions oppose age discrimination and have reached an agreement with the government by which both teenage and adult minimum will be equalized by 1998. At the start of 1994, apprenticeship contracts were introduced for workers under the age of 25. These contracts must be between six months and three years in length and allow the employer to pay 70% of the SMI in the first year, 80% in the second and 90% in the third. Unemployment and health benefits are not included and they can be used by firms with less than 25 employees. However, according to the new labour market reform to be signed by unions and employers federations, they will be replaced by training contracts whose wage corresponds to 85% of the minimum wage in the first year. Furthermore, as in some other countries, the levels of some welfare benefits are linked to the minimum wage. For example, unemployment assistance (paid after entitlement to unemployment insurance has been exhausted) is generally 75% of the SMI (and 100% (125%) for unemployed heads of households aged 45 or more with 2 (2 or more) dependent relatives). Obviously, this makes it very difficult to disentangle the effects of benefits from those of the minimum wage per se.

The purpose of this section is to present briefly descriptive evidence on the size and incidence of the SMI. In this sense, we may highlight the following points:

(i) The use of the Kaitz index – the ratio of the minimum wage to average earnings – to analyse its relative size, shows that it has been trending downward since its introduction. Figure 7.1 represents the trends of Kaitz indices for the SMI, since 1964. Three Kaitz indices are presented in the figure, corresponding to each type of minimum wage in force until 1990: for those workers aged 18 or over (18+), 17-year-olds (17) and younger than 17 workers (17-).

Figure 7.1
Kaitz indices for different age groups

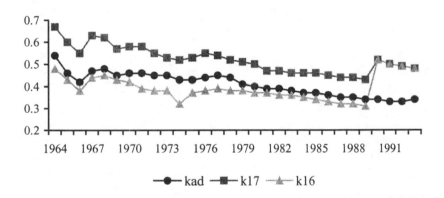

Note: kad is the adult Kaitz index; k17 the Kaitz index for 17-year-olds and k16 the Kaitz index for those aged less than 17.

Source: Encuesta de Salarios.

Average wages have been computed for the different age groups, so that even though minimum rates for groups (17) and (17-) are clearly below that for adults, their corresponding indices can be larger if their average wage is much lower. This is the case for the Kaitz index for (17) which is about two percentage points above that for (18+) workers during the sample period. Apart from the downward trend in all the indices until 1990, the most noticeable feature is the increase in the minimum wage for workers aged 16 that took place in 1990. In that year, wages for the two teenagers' groups were homogenized into a single one. That meant a substantial increase (83%)

in the minimum wage of the (17-) workers, at the time that for the intermediate group (17) it was raised 15%, in a year in which the inflation rate was only 6.5%. We will study this episode in more detail below.

Table 7.1:
Distribution of wage earners comparing their earnings with the SMI

	Wage < SMI	Wage = SMI	Wage> SMI
All workers	5.5	5.7	88.8
Primary sector	9.0	9.9	81.1
Industry	2.5	3.2	94.5
Construction	4.3	7.0	88.6
Services	7.1	6.6	86.4
Female	10.3	9.1	80.6
Male	2.8	3.8	93.4
Age < 20	17.8	28.3	53.6
Age 20–24	12.2	11.2	76.7
Age 25–29	4.8	5.5	89.7
Age 30–54	3.1	3.9	93.0
Age > 54	6.3	2.3	91.3
Firm size:			
< 6 employees	15.2	15.6	69.2
6–10 employees	9.4	5.2	85.4
11–20 employees	6.4	5.4	88.2
> 20 employees	2.2	2.5	95.3
Temporary and/or part-time			
Contracts	9.5	10.6	79.9
Other types of contracts	3.3	3.0	93.7
Overtime work journey	19.4	15.0	65.6
Ordinary work journey	2.6	3.8	93.5

It should be noted that due to the national nature of the statutory minimum wage in Spain, all its variability will stem from its time variability without any cross-sectional variation, for instance by sectors or regions, as is the case in other countries. Therefore, the size of changes as those described above will help in evaluating the effects of changes in the minimum wages on employment. In particular, those increases have implied a substantial rise in the proportion between the youths' and adults' minimum wage that has gone from 40% before 1990 to 77% in 1995. Consistently the (17-) workers Kaitz index has increased from 0.30 before 1990 to 0.53 after that year. By 1997, in agreement with the progressive convergence of teenage minimum wage to the adult level, the ratio reached 89%. In this sense, the preliminary descriptive evidence seems to point to the fact that, if there exists any negative effect on employment, it will tend to be more noticeable in the case of young workers.

(ii) Regarding the percentage of workers who perceive the SMI, the use of tax withholding data sources (DART) lead us to infer a proportion of 6.6% in 1989 (see Melis and Díaz, 1995). However, this measure of the incidence of the SMI corresponds to the 'spike' of an annual earnings distribution, without any information about the number of working days. A more reliable data source to evaluate the proportion of minimum wage earners is the *Class Structure, Consciousness and Biography Survey* (ECBC, 1991) where both earnings and working time are reported by a representative sample of employees. A simple comparison of the hourly earnings declared by each individual and its equivalent in terms of the SMI reveals that 5.7% of paid workers perceived the latter. However, we have to highlight that a significant proportion of individuals (5.5%) declare that they earn less than the SMI, indicating the presence of an irregular segment of the labour market that hides the potential number of employees to which the SMI was initially directed – and thus limits its possible redistributive nature. This feature takes place among individuals, firms and sectors in which a greater propensity to irregularities is expected. In Table 7.1, we show the distribution of wage earners according to the ECBC, comparing their earnings with the SMI. As it can be observed, the segment of workers that declares a wage below the minimum is particularly relevant in the primary and service sectors, among women and youths, with a temporary and/or part-time contract, in small-size firms and among those who extend the daily work journey above the legal one.

(iii) In Table 7.2, using the information from various sources, we show an estimation of the sectoral distribution of the earners of the minimum wage in the 1990s, as well as some of their socio-demographic characteristics, and finally, the proportion of existing earners in each decile of the household income distribution. When comparing the sectoral distribution of total paid workers and minimum wage earners, we observe that the latter tend to be overrepresented in the service sector, particularly in sectors such as trade, restaurants, hotel trade and other services. On the other hand, 60% of the earners are women; 40% of the total is made up by young workers (16–24), while earners with temporary/part-time contracts represent about 60–70%. Therefore, in contrast to the conventional wisdom based on the fact that the effects of the minimum wages are concentrated on youths, the previous

Individual Country Experiences

evidence seems to indicate that the typical portrait of the earners in Spain is that of a woman, older than 20, with some type of an irregular contract, and that even in some cases can be head of the household. This impression is partially supported by the information contained in the third part of Table

Table 7.2:
Sectoral distribution and socio-demographic characteristics
of the minimum wage earners*

	DART-EDS		ECBC	
	Total wage earners	Minimum wage earners	Total wage earners	Minimum wage earners
1. *Sectoral distribution*				
Primary sector	-	-	3.8	6.6
Manufacturing	23.5	9.9	27.1	16.2
Construction	9.0	8.8	8.5	10.6
Service sector	67.3	81.3	57.8	66.6
2. *Gender, age and type of contract*				
Female	31.1	58.0	35.7	56.9
Age < 20 years	3.1	12.3	2.1	10.2
Age 20-24 years	10.2	28.7	16.3	32.0
Temporary and/or part-time contract	29.6	57.0	35.7	68.7
3. *Position of the minimum wage earners in the income distribution per household*				
Decile				
1	-	35.5	-	-
2	-	18.4	-	-
3	-	14.5	-	-
8	-	2.0	-	-
9	-	0.9	-	-
10	-	0.2	-	-

* Percentage share of each group over total wage and minimum wage earners.

7.2 which shows the position of minimum wage earners in the income distribution per household, adjusting the number of children in each household by the Oxford method. As we move to the upper deciles, we observe that the proportion of earners decreases drastically, so that they are concentrated in the households with the lowest resources. Therefore, the belief that earners do not belong to poor households does not seem to hold, since 70% of them are concentrated in the three lower deciles of the distribution. Accordingly, the redistributive role of the minimum wage may be potentially important if it is effective and its effects on employment are not excessively negative, issues that will be considered below.

(iv) Although the above measures are clearly imperfect, they are useful to provide a comparison of the Spanish experience with those in other countries. In this way, Table 7.3 reports Kaitz indices and an estimate of the 'spike' for a set of OECD countries during the 1990s, distinguishing between those countries where a minimum wage is set at a national level and those where it is only fixed as part of the collective bargaining. Besides, in those countries where it is available, we offer a relative measure of the youth minimum wage as a proportion of that for adults. We observe that the Kaitz index in Spain (35%) is on a level with that of the United States, and below the existing level in most European countries – around 50% to 70%. Nevertheless, the existence of sectoral minimum wages in countries like Germany and Italy, where the highest minimum wage can triple the lowest, makes comparisons difficult. With regard to the percentage of affected workers – around 6% – we can assert that it is in line with the existing one in most of the remaining countries, with the exception of France (11%) and other economies with greater an agricultural intensity than the Spanish, like Greece (20%) and Portugal (8%). As regards the youth minimum wage, the results are again similar, although, as we have already seen, the gap between their wage and the adult minimum wage has significantly narrowed during the last years.

(v) Such a low fraction of SMI earners and Kaitz index cannot be well understood without a brief reference to the role played by collective bargaining in the wage-determination process in Spain. We do not intend to go into detail on a subject that has been the object of many studies. Nevertheless, we will try to address the following question: what is the margin left to the SMI by collective bargaining?

The SMI and the rates fixed in collective agreements are closely related to the so-called principle of application of the most beneficial labour norm to the worker. Following this principle, labour contracts must stipulate labour conditions which are at least as beneficial to the worker as the ones agreed at the immediately superior level of collective agreement or, if there is not any, it must adjust to the minimum conditions fixed by the government. The earnings of all wage earners have thus a guaranteed 'floor' which can be determined by a sectoral or activity branch agreement with a local, regional or national scope, or by the labour laws that regulate these issues. The coexistence of two types of minimum wage, the SMI and those agreed at sectoral collective bargaining, constitutes an important feature of the Spanish labour market. Moreover, other characteristics, such as the *principle of general effectiveness* or *erga omnes* (according to which, the agreed conditions affect all workers and firms in their scope of bargaining, irrespective of whether they are union members or not) and the requirements needed in order to be able to bargain collective agreements above the level of the firm, are essential characteristics to explain the high coverage of collective agreements: 85% of the wage earners.

Table 7.3:
Minimum wages in the OECD countries

Country	Kaitz index	Minimum wage earners (%)	Youth minimum wage/ Adult minimum wage
[National minimum wage]			
Australia	0.35 (1992)	5.0	--
Belgium	0.60 (1992)	4.0	0.90 (<23)
Spain	**0.35 (1994)**	**5.0**	**0.66 (<18)**
France	0.50 (1993)	11.0	0.80–0.90 (<17)
Greece	0.62 (1995)	20.0	1.00
Netherlands	0.55 (1993)	3.5	0.70 (<21)
Portugal	0.45 (1993)	8.0	0.75 (<18)
USA	0.33 (1993)	4.0	1.00
[Collective bargaining/Wage councils]			
Germany	0.55 (1991)	--	--
Austria	0.62 (1993)	4.0	--
Denmark	0.54 (1994)	6.0	0.40 (<18)
Ireland	0.55 (1993)	--	0.60–0.80 (<21)
Italy	0.71 (1991)	--	--
UK	0.40 (1993)	--	0.00
Sweden	0.52 (1992)	0.2	0.85 (<24)

Source: Dolado *et al.* (1996) and Freeman (1996).

Then two questions arise: (i) What are the characteristics of the wage earners that constitute the remaining 15%? and, (ii) Are the agreed rates really larger than the SMI? Unfortunately, there are no official data sources that enable us to answer these questions. Thus, the only solution is to design our own data base, from a random sample of collective agreements. In particular, for this study we have gathered information on the remuneration agreed in sectoral collective agreements which were in force in December of 1990, in the industrial, construction, trade and hotel business sectors.

Figure 7.2a
Differences between agreed minimum wages and the SMI
(age 16–17)

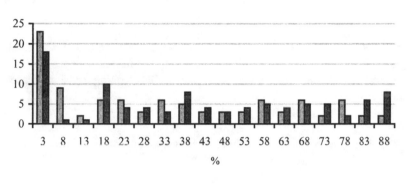

Figure 7.2b
Differences between agreed minimum wages and the SMI
(workers older than 18)

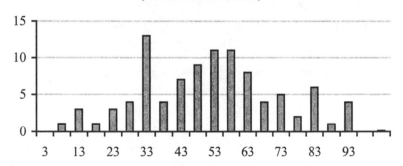

The first type of information we get from this data base is the one concerning the type of wage earner affected by collective bargaining. In this sense, we can highlight that, apart from executive positions – whose working conditions are regulated outside the agreements – the categories that appear the highest up in the agreements are those corresponding to highly skilled workers (for example, graduates, which only show up in 55% of the wages tables), subject to other informal agreements with the firm. Hence, if a high proportion of the 15% is made up by qualified workers – not affected by the SMI – we can conclude that the proportion of covered workers must be smaller, leaving a lower margin than expected to the effectiveness of the SMI as a wage distribution 'floor'. As regards the workers under 18, although they show up in 75% of the tables, in most of the cases they just appear symbolically to indicate that their minimum agreed rates coincide with the SMI. Figures 7.2a, and 7.2b represent the histograms of the differences between the lowest annual agreed rates in the sectoral collective agreements and the SMI for teenagers and adults, respectively. As can be observed, in the first two figures, the wage floor corresponding to 22.5% and 18% of the 16- and 17-year-old workers in the chosen sectors is basically the SMI. In the case of workers older than 18, however, the minimum wages agreed in sectoral agreements are higher than the SMI, reaching in some cases a difference of 120%.

Figure 7.3

Differences between agreed minimum wages and the SMI (by sectors)
(adults)

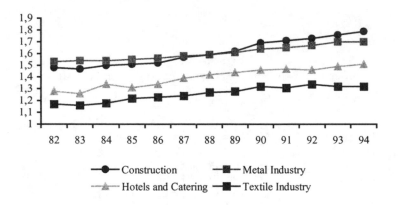

In Figure 7.3, the agreed rates in the period 1982–94 are depicted, based on information on collectively agreed wage increases. As can be observed, in all the chosen sectors, the wedge between the minimum rate for workers above 18 and the SMI has been continuously rising throughout the period. For example, in the textile sector, where according to the Earnings Survey, the lowest wages are paid, the so-called 'minimum intertextile wage' with a national scope, has been 30% above the SMI since the beginning of the 1990s. In sum, it seems that the relevant 'wage floors' are those agreed in collective bargaining.

(vi) Since our analysis ends in 1994, we have not picked up the effects of the last legal reform in 1994, that affects both the collective bargaining and the potential SMI earners by means of the apprenticeship and training contracts. In fact, the law establishes that in both types of contract, the collective agreements can set the corresponding wage below the SMI, unless it is determined otherwise. In this sense, a preliminary evaluation of the effects of the 1994 reform reveals that only a small proportion of this type of contract were in force in December 1995 (about 200 000 out of 8 million contracts, i.e. 2.5%), and for those which were signed, the corresponding agreed minimum rates were much higher than the legal minimum rates.

3   EMPIRICAL APPROACHES

There is a wide range of empirical approaches in the literature when it comes to estimating the effects of minimum wages on employment. In what follows, we summarize four procedures, which underlie the empirical evidence that will be discussed in section 4.

In the first place, a frequently used approach consists in regressing employment changes on the minimum wage, controlling for the possible effect of other relevant factors through the estimate of a reduced form employment equation, as a function of wages, and wages as a function of the minimum wage. This approach typically exploits changes in the minimum wage, through the Kaitz index, either along time or across sectors and regions. Its interpretation is intuitively simple, although it is subject to several criticisms. Then, if changes in demand of supply factors are not adequately controlled for, the estimations of the effects on employment may be biased. A second criticism focuses on the possible endogeneity of the minimum wage – it is argued that it increases in the upward stages of the cycle – that would imply the search for suitable instrumental variables.

A second approach that has recently become popular is the exploitation of the so-called 'natural experiments'. This is the case of the controversial study by Card and Krueger (1994), who study the effects of an increase in the hourly minimum wage in New Jersey in April 1994, choosing as a control group the state of Pennsylvania, where the minimum wage remained unchanged. Unfortunately, this method is not directly applicable to countries like Spain, where the minimum wage is national, so that there is no cross-section variability by region or sector. There are, however, control groups that can be used in this case, giving rise to the so-called 'differential impact' approach. For example, there are regions, sectors or occupations where the proportion of workers with low wages are higher, so that the impact of an increase in the minimum wage will be more intense for these groups. An analysis of this kind, using information related to the large shift of the youth minimum wage in 1990 will be discussed later.

A third approach that also enjoys some popularity is that developed by Meyer and Wise (1983a,b). They try to infer the effect of minimum wages on wages and employment using the information on the wage distribution for a particular period. To do this, we assume a certain functional form for the wage distribution in the absence of a minimum wage (e.g., the log-normal distribution) and we establish a threshold in the distribution above which workers' wages would not be affected by variations in the minimum wage. Next, the parameters of the truncated distribution, belonging to non-covered workers, are estimated. If we are using aggregate data, the estimated parameters allow us to infer the proportion of workers who either earn the minimum wage or who are below it in the hypothetical labour market. Finally, we can compare that theoretical proportion with the one that really exists in the prevailing wage distribution. If the latter is lower than the former, this would be an indication of a negative effect of the minimum wage on employment.

A number of difficulties arise from the possible lack of robustness when we change the initial assumptions about the functional form and the chosen threshold (see Dickens *et al.*, 1994). Another type of analysis, closer in spirit to the original model of Meyer and Wise, focuses on estimating the individual wage gains that arise from the setting of the minimum wage. We can then proceed to estimate the wage that an employed individual can expect in the hypothetical labour market, and compare it with the wage that can be expected in the current labour market. To do so, we need to classify the individuals in terms of their current earnings: whether they are larger, equal to or less than the minimum wage, or simply null (because he/she is unemployed), and to find out the probabilities of being in each of these situations, before and after the minimum wage was set. To do so, we have to use individual data on the socio-demographic and labour market characteristics for a sample of wage earners. The merit of this approach lies in that it considers the individual effects of minimum wages on current wages, that cannot be considered if we are working with aggregate data. However, this model does not allow for a positive effect of the minimum wage on employment (monopsony). In the next section we will discuss an application of this approach to the Spanish economy.

Finally, a fourth approach is based on the so-called 'disequilibrium' methodology (see Neumark and Wascher, 1994). The basic idea consists in using an econometric procedure of switching regression models to estimate the probability of being in each of three following regimes: i) a regime in which the minimum wage is not operative as it is below the monopsony wage; ii) a supply regime where the minimum wage is between the monopsony wage and the competitive wage; and iii) a regime in which the minimum wage is operative and employment is set in terms of the value of the marginal product, that is, the minimum wage is above the competitive wage. We will discuss an exercise of this kind in the next section.

4   RESULTS

In the light of the methods described in the previous section, we proceed to discuss four exercises directed to evaluate the effects of the minimum wage on employment and on the wage distribution. In the two first exercises, the evidence will be based on the results we obtained in other studies, so that the discussion will be brief. In the third one, we will make a comparison between the results obtained by applying the Meyer and Wise approach to examining the effects of the SMI on wages, and another one that applies the same methodology to the guaranteed remuneration in sectoral agreements. Finally, the last exercise, corresponding to the 'disequilibrium' methodology, is an original contribution of the present paper, so we will deal with it in more detail.

(i) Dolado *et al.* (1996) estimate the effects of the minimum wage on employment through a reduced form employment equation. To do so, we regress the rate of change of the employment on the rate of change of the Kaitz index and other variables trying to control for the changes in the factors shifting the labour supply and demand curves. These control variables are the growth rates of the sectoral GDP and hours, total GDP, as well as the rate of productive capacity utilization, with the purpose of controlling for cyclical factors. We use a panel made up of the six sectors, for the 1967–94 period. The estimated elasticities of employment with respect to the Kaitz index are 0.082 (t-ratio = 1.38) in the case of total employment, 0.063 (t-ratio = 1.22) in the case of young adult group (20–24) and -0.154 (t-ratio = -1.65) in the case of teenagers (16–19). These results, very similar to those obtained by Pérez Domínguez (1995), are in line with the conventional wisdom about youth employment, though they are among the low range of elasticities estimated in the literature, between -0.1 and -0.3. Nevertheless, this is not the case for total employment, whose estimated elasticity is practically zero. The latter effect may be due to progressive substitution of young workers by adult ones due to relative increase in their minimum wage along the sample period.

(ii) In order to test the previous hypothesis, Dolado *et al.* (1996) use the differential impact methodology, making use of the drastic rise in youth minimum wage in 1990. If there exists a negative impact on youth employment, we would expect that the largest unfavourable effect would be suffered by those regions with a greater proportion of workers with low wages, measured by the proportion of workers in each region whose wages are below 60% of the median regional wage. In Figure 7.4a, we observe that employment of the group between 16–19 declined more during the period following the rise. In Figure 7.4b we can see that the opposite effect holds for the 20–24 group. As pointed out before, a possible explanation for these results would be consistent with the substitution of adult workers for youth-teenagers.

Figure 7.4a
Changes in teenage employment rates in Spanish regions, 1990–1994

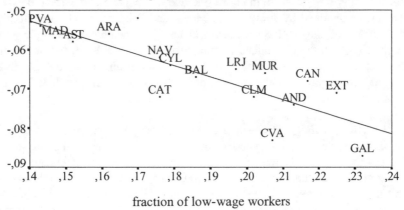

fraction of low-wage workers

Figure 7.4b
Changes in adult employment rates in Spanish regions, 1990–1994

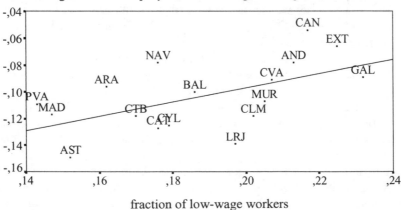

fraction of low-wage workers

Table 7.4:
Underlying wage function and wage gains, for workers aged 18–24
(Meyer and Wise approach)

Underlying wage function				
Variables	Coeff.	(t-ratio)	Wage earners	Wage gains (%)
Constant	5.61	(43.95)	All workers	0.35
School	0.04	(4.49)		
Tenure	0.01	(0.98)	Male	0.20
Gender (1=Male)	0.18	(3.23)	Female	0.56
Agriculture	0.03	(-0.15)		
Industry1	0.07	(-0.84)	Tenure = 1 year	0.40
Industry2	-0.23	(-3.05)	Tenure= 4 years	0.30
Construction	0.03	(0.30)		
Services1	-0.20	(-3.41)	Agriculture	0.23
Castilla-León	-0.02	(-0.11)	Industry1	0.31
Cataluña	0.30	(3.91)	Industry2	0.70
Galicia	0.03	(0.16)	Construction	0.15
Madrid	0.18	(1.76)	Services1	0.62
País Vasco	0.41	(4.71)	Services2	0.20
Cornisa	-0.02	(-0.19)		
Cantábrica	0.09	(0.79)	Andalucía	0.58
Ebro	0.05	(0.49)	Castilla-León	0.64
Meseta	-0.03	(-0.48)	Cataluña	0.07
Levante	-0.02	(-.19)	Galicia	0.51
Islas	0.37	(25.34)	Madrid	0.20
			País Vasco	0.01
P1	0.87	(3.13)	Cornisa Cantábrica	0.62
P3	-0.12	(0.02)	Ebro	0.37
			Meseta	0.45
Log Likelihood	-208.7		Levante	0.67
N	366		Islas	0.64

Notes: Industry1 = mining, chemical and   metal industry; Industry2 = other manufacturing; Services1 = commerce, hotel and catering; Services2 = other services; P1, probability that a subminimum worker is paid below the SMI because of noncompliance; P3, probability that a subminimum worker is paid the SMI.

(iii) The two previous exercises seem to suggest that the minimum wage has had a negative albeit small effect on the teenage employment in Spain. However, for the young-adult group (20–24), the evidence suggests that the effect has been null or even positive. The aim of the following exercises is to check whether that evidence can be related with a positive genuine 'monopsony effect.'

Individual Country Experiences

Table 7.5:
Labour supply and marginal product value functions
(Neumark and Wascher – disequilibrium approach)

Variables	Teenagers (16–19)		Young adults (20–24)	
	Estim. Coef.	t-ratio	Estim. coef.	t-ratio
Mpv function:				
Constant	-0.04	(-6.12)	0.00	(0.16)
Employment rate 16–19	-0.06	(-10.21)		
Employment rate 20–24			-0.06	(-3.83)
Employment rate > 24			0.04	(2.88)
Employment rate > 19	0.03	(11.92)		
Inverse supply function:				
Constant	0.03	(7.66)	0.01	(2.59)
Employment rate 16–19	0.02	(10.21)		
Employment rate 20–24			0.01	(3.83)
n	0.24	(9.25)	0.22	(3.91)
a	0.06	(1.62)	0.20	(2.19)
an	0.01	(0.01)	0.04	(1.78)
b	0.77	(8.93)	0.38	(4.18)
bn	-0.05	(-2.16)	-0.06	(-2.32)
m	0.13	(22.81)	0.11	(23.03)
mn	0.03	(7.42)	-0.22	(-3.95)
Log Likelihood	-688.87		-214.7	
N.	459		459	

Notes: Other control variables are a time trend and regional dummies in the mpv function, and quarterly dummies in the inverse labour supply function.

Obviously, a necessary condition for minimum wages to have any effect on employment is to be above the wage that would prevail in its absence. Consequently, we should try to find some measure of the difference between the current remuneration of the workers and the one that they would receive if there was no minimum wage. To do so, we estimate the 'wage-gain', that is, the difference between the wages expected by an individual in the presence and in the absence of minimum wages. The methodology chosen to do so is based on the Meyer and Wise (1983a,b) approach. For this purpose, we use a subsample of the ECBC, composed of a group of wage earners aged between 18 and 24, with the purpose of concentrating on the effects of the minimum wage on the youngest group of workers, in order to confirm the previous results.

Figure 7.5a

Probabilities of each regime in the monopsony model, by region
(teenagers)

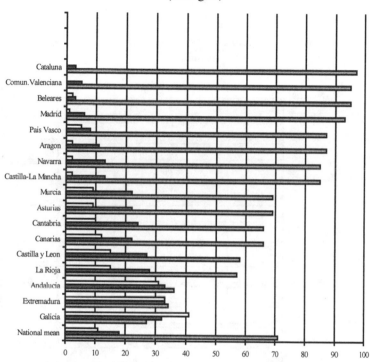

☐ Pr (Non-binding regime)   ◼ Pr (Supply regime)   ☐ Pr (Demand regime)

The results are reported in Table 7.4, where we show the estimates of the latent wage function (in the absence of minima) in terms of such variables as the degree of schooling, tenure, sex, sector and region, as well as the estimates of the wage gains for the whole sample. The most important result, apart from the appropiate of the signs of the education and sex variables and the lack of significance of tenure, is that the estimated wage gains are practically null in all cases. These results contrast with those obtained by Dolado *et al.* (1997) in a similar exercise, where they use as minimum wage the wage floors fixed in the corresponding sectoral agreement, instead of SMI. In this case, the wage gains obtained for the (18–24) group of workers range between 13% and 17%. Everything thus seems to indicate that, in general terms, the really operative minimum wage in the Spanish labour market is that fixed in the sectoral collective agreements. Therefore, given the lack of operativeness of the SMI, we cannot associate it with a possible 'monopsony effect' on employment of this age group of age, as we conjectured on the basis of the results previously obtained.

Figure 7.5b

Probabilities of each regime in the monopsony model, by region
(adults)

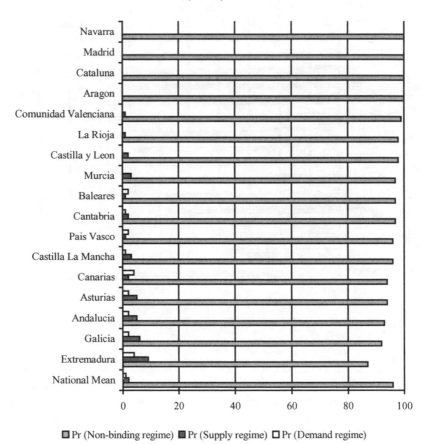

□ Pr (Non-binding regime) ▨ Pr (Supply regime) □ Pr (Demand regime)

(iv) Although the disequilibrium method suggested by Neumark and Wascher (1994) fails to use individual data, it allows for a classification on the degree of operativeness of the minimum wage, as well as for testing the degree of monopsony in the labour market. In this exercise, whose details can be consulted in the Appendix, we estimate the marginal product value and the inverse supply function, using quarterly data on regional unemployment from the Spanish Labour Force Survey (EPA) and on wage from the Earnings Survey, between 1989:1 and 1995:3. The results are conclusive and tend to confirm the ones achieved in the previous exercises.

Figure 7.6a
Probabilities of each regime in the monopsony model (1989–1995)

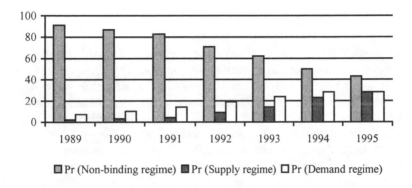

□ Pr (Non-binding regime) ■ Pr (Supply regime) □ Pr (Demand regime)

Figure 7.6b
Probabilities of each regime in the monopsony model (1989–1995)
(adults)

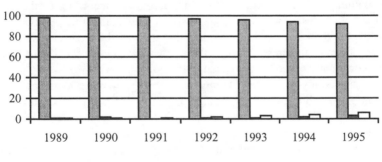

□ Pr (Non-binding regime) ■ Pr (Supply regime) □ Pr (Demand regime)

We find that the probability of an observation lying on the demand regime is substantial in some regions [Galicia (41%), Extremadura and Andalucía (more than 30%)]. In the remaining regions, however, the prevailing regime is still that of the non operativeness. If we compare these results with those in Figure 7.5a, we can confirm that the regions with a high probability of being in a demand regime are the ones that influence the negative slope to be very steep. It is also important to highlight how the probability of non-operativeness for teenagers has fallen greatly along the period, going from 91% in 1989 to 43% in 1995, which implies an increasing effectiveness of the SMI. For the 20–24 group things are quite different, rejecting the possibility of a monopsony effect during the chosen period.

5. CONCLUSIONS

Economists like to attack old ideas, apparently well founded and adopted by a great part of the profession, but that stagger when any of the key assumptions that support them are questioned. Legislation on minimum wages and their effects on employment has become, once again, one of the star subjects on both sides of the Atlantic. In the United States and Great Britain, the question has emerged following the strong deterioration experienced in the wage distribution during the last decade. In Europe, the new interest for this is related to the sever losses of low-qualification jobs that took place over the last decades. For both reasons, the role played by the minimum wage has occupied again a prominent place in the agenda of policy makers and in the research projects of academics. The state of affairs can be summarized as follows. Opposite to the traditional view that a minimum wage has harmful effects on employment, there has emerged a trend in opinion that argues that this is possibly not the case. This is because it is argued that the underlying assumption – the functioning of the labour market according to the perfect competition rules – far from adequately represents the real functioning of that market. On the other hand, it is argued that the possibility of the existence of monopsonistic features in the labour market goes beyond the simple theoretical curiosity to become a tangible reality.

In this study we have attempted to bring forward evidence on the potentiality of both trends of thought in the Spanish case, focusing on the impact of the statutory minimum wage on the youth employment. Among the main results we can highlight the following:

(i) Since its establishment in the 60s, the SMI has declined substantially in proportion to the average wage, while its incidence does not exceed 5% or 6% of wage earners nowadays.

(ii) It is, therefore, hard to argue that the setting of the SMI has been one of the main causes of the deficient evolution of employment in Spain. In the case of the SMI for workers over 18 (adults) the results point to the fact that its effect on employment is basically null, either because there is a certain segment of the black economy with retribution under the legal minima or because the binding wage floors of this type of worker are the wage rates arising from sectoral collective agreements.

(iii) In the case of teenage workers, however, the results show the existence of a negative relationship between the SMI and employment, finding that a 10% increase in the SMI can reduce employment of that group in between 1% and 3%. This negative effect has not been homogeneous across regions. In particular, those regions with a greater proportion of low wage workers have been more affected by the negative impact of the recent increases in the youth SMI.

(iv) Even though a great part of the discussion around the minimum wages focuses on the effects on youth employment, the features of the typical minimum wage earner in Spain are changing. They are shifting from a young and inexperienced worker to more adult people, predominantly women, with temporary and/or part-time contracts, living in households with scarce resources.

(v) The evidence showed that the elasticity of employment with respect to the SMI is clearly lower than unity (null for adults and -0.2 for youth) which would give the SMI a certain redistributive power. Nonetheless, the evidence of a strong degree of non-compliance of the legal rules and the lack of evidence of the effects of increases in the SMI on the labour supply and on the fixing of minimum agreed wages, makes it very risky to recommend a large upward revision of SMI. In any case, the message of our study is that the SMI concerning the adult workers has not been operative and so it cannot be interpreted as a signal of success or failure of the Spanish labour market.

(vi) Finally, in light of the obtained results, a few words about the recent decision of the government to raise the adult minimum wage by 2.6% in 1997 – against the unions' proposal of a 7.1% increase to catch up some of the foregone purchasing power over the last decade – while the teenage minimum wage was raised by 17.7% and there is a commitment to equalize them by 1998. According to the results presented in this paper, both decisions seem to be wrong. Whilst the unions' proposal could have been accepted without any cut in jobs, the staggering increase in the teenage minimum will have unfavourable effects on youth employment, whose unemployment rate already reaches 48%. If the reason for denying the unions' petition is a budgetary one (unemployment benefits and other subsidies are linked to the level of minimum wages) then the easiest way is to break those links, introducing in-work-benefits to avoid people falling into a 'poverty trap'.

REFERENCES

Card, D. and Krueger, A. (1994), 'Minimum wages and employment: a case study of the fast food industry in New Jersey and Pennsylvania', *American*

Economic Review, **84**, 772–793.

Card, D. and Krueger, A. (1995), *Myth and Measurement: The New Economics of the Minimum Wage*, Princeton, Princeton University Press.

Dickens, R., Machin, S. and Manning, A. (1994), Estimating the effect of minimum wages on employment from the distribution of wages: a critical review, LSE/CEP Discussion Paper 203.

Dolado, J., *et al.*(1996), 'The economic impact of minimum wages in Europe', *Economic Policy*, **23**, 317–372.

Dolado, J. and Felgueroso, F. (1997) : 'Los efectos del salario mínimo : evidencia empírica para el caso español', *Moneda y Crédito*, **204**, 213–261.

Dolado, J., Felgueroso, F. and J. Jimeno (1997), 'The effects of minimum bargained wages on earnings: evidence from Spain', *European Economic chin, S. and Manning, A. (1996): 'Employment and the introduction of a minimum wage in Britain', *Economic Journal*, **106**, 667–673. *Review*, **41**, 713–721.

Dolado, J. ; Kramarz, F. ; Machin, S. ; Manning, A ; Margolis, D. and Teulings, C. (1996) : "The economic impact of minimum wages in Europe", *Economic Policy*, 23, 317-372.

ECBC (1991), *Encuesta de Estructura, Conciencia y Biografía de Clase*, Comunidad de Madrid, Madrid.

Freeman, R.B: (1996): "The minimum wage as a redistributive tool", *Economic Journal*, 106, 639-649.

Machin, S. and Manning, A. (1996): 'Employment and the introduction of a minimum wage in Britain', *Economic Journal*, **106**, 667–673.

Melis, F. and Díaz, C. (1995), 'La distribución personal de salarios y pensiones en las fuentes tributarias', *Informe Argentaria sobre Distribución de la Renta*, 151–169.

Meyer, R. and Wise, D. (1983a), 'Discontinuous distributions and missing persons: the minimum wage and unemployed youth', *Econometrica*, **61**, 1677–1698.

Meyer, R. and Wise, D. (1983b), 'The effects of the minimum wage on the employment and earnings of youth', *Journal of Labour Economics*, **1**, 66–100.

Neumark, D. and Wascher, W. (1994), 'Minimum wage effects and low-wage labor markets: a disequilibrium approach', NBER Working Paper 4617.

Pérez Domínguez, C. (1995), 'Los efectos del Salario Mínimo sobre el empleo y el desempleo: evidencia empírica para España', Mimeo, Universidad de Valladolid.

PART THREE

Low Pay Among School-Leavers

8. Sub-Minimum-Wage Employment, Earnings Profiles and Wage Mobility in the Low-Skill Youth Labour Market: Evidence from French Panel Data 1989–95

Didier Balsan, Saïd Hanchane and Patrick Werquin

---

1   INTRODUCTION: THE FRENCH CONTEXT

Youth employment rates in France have suffered a sharp and continuing decline for the last two decades. Young people entering the labour market are particularly vulnerable, and long-term unemployment is excluding greater and greater portions of young workers from the labour market[1]. To solve these problems the government has developed multiple labour market training programme (Werquin, 1997) for young people with low academic levels as an alternative to traditional school: to give them a better idea of their abilities, permitting them to learn about the world of work and helping them to make the transition towards employment. This very often gives a misleading view of the earnings distribution in France: fixed term contracts, temporary and marginal jobs exist alongside regular ones. Associated wages thus range from the poverty line[2] level (2500 French francs per month) to much higher levels.

If more and more people are continuing their studies, some exit school before getting their 'baccalauréat'[3] (bac for short). For them, the period of transition from school to work has become longer and the process of mobility on the labour market has become more complicated (Balsan *et al.*, 1996). It is therefore inadequate to analyse entry into the labour market by comparing unemployment rates, etc. A more dynamic process should be considered taking into account job duration, job tenure and job sequences. Differences between the various jobs are based on the type of work contracts,

151

particularly fixed-term and unlimited duration contracts. The latter was the norm for employment until the 1970s. Given the climate of recession, firms have developed new forms of work contracts (fixed term contracts, temporary positions) in order to gain more flexibility. This has led to an increase in the number of precarious jobs. A job will be termed precarious when the probability of losing his/her job is high and the duration of the job is short. The term 'precariousness' will then refer to a sequence of precarious jobs so that there will be alternating periods of unemployment, short-term employment and return to unemployment and maybe even a stage when the individual leaves the labour force (some workers can become discouraged, for example). In addition, it is likely that there will be a clear link between 'precariousness' and work contracts. It is therefore of great importance to take a look at the itineraries of the young people who exit school with a low academic level. Do they only obtain precarious jobs? How does it affect their income? Will there be differences between male and female workers?

The main focus of the paper is low pay among pre-bac-level young people in the six-year period which follows initial education. The paper ranges from descriptive statistics to more complex econometric models where the major variables come from individual characteristics or labour market history.

First of all, the determinants of wages for early school-leavers (supposedly low-skilled) are estimated and analysed (section 2). In section 3 the issue of wage mobility is then addressed using panel data techniques. A non-linear model is estimated to figure out, how, simultaneously, young people move between non-employment – studies, schemes, unemployment, out of labour force – to employment and to identify an upward or downward movement in wages when some mobility is observed within employment.

2   THE DETERMINANTS OF WAGES FOR LOW-LEVEL LEAVERS IN FRANCE

This section addresses two main issues. First of all, the existence of a minimum wage in France deserves some specific attention regarding the way the regulation is made and implemented. Then a wage equation is estimated for low-level school-leavers.

Youth Wages are Distributed around the Minimum Wage

In France, there is a legal minimum wage for all occupations. It is called SMIC (Salaire minimum interprofessionnel de croissance). Some collective agreements may improve the value of the SMIC and the Ministry of Labour may extend the existence of these collectively-determined minimum wages to sectors where it does not exist. In 1990, the value of the hourly SMIC was approximately 26 french francs net of social security contributions (around 4400 francs per month). The SMIC is meaningful for studying youth programmes since it serves as a benchmark for almost all wages paid.

Figure 8.1

Female hourly wage from 1990 to 1995 in constant prices (regular jobs)

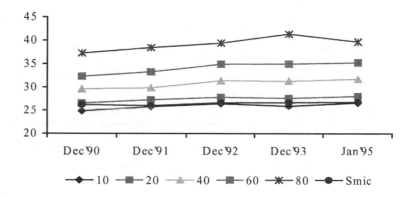

Figure 8.2

Male hourly wage from 1990 to 1995 in constant prices (regular jobs)

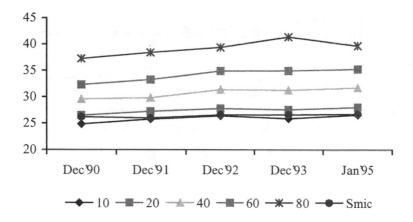

Inspection of Figures 8.1 to 8.4[4] and, as we follow the cohort under study on the labour market by gender, reveals that the five fractiles increase by a very small proportion over six years. This proves to be constant even when observing deciles. These pieces of evidence suggest that either the situation is

Low Pay Among School-Leavers

very stable for all the young people – very few of them do actually move from a portion of the wage distribution to another – or when some earn more, others earn less – so the overall impression is one of stability.

Figure 8.3

Female hourly wage from 1990 to 1995 in constant prices (youth schemes)

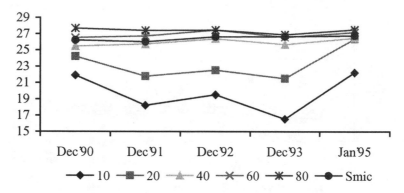

Figure 8.4

Male hourly wage from 1990 to 1995 in constant prices (youth schemes)

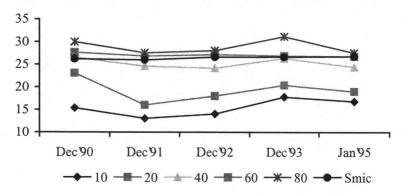

One more important result is that a fair proportion of low-skilled young people earn less than the minimum wage (SMIC). Indeed, the breakdown by gender shows that 20% of the women and about 10 % of the men are below minimum. This piece of evidence is not straightforward because (a) we have excluded individuals in special youth employment schemes and (b) we use hourly wages which means the part timer effect is removed. One would expect to observe wages above minimum for young people in regular jobs and wages below minimum for those entering a youth programme. Even with all these precautions taken, there are still possible measurement errors which can explain this discrepancy between the expected and the actual distribution. The errors may come from a mismeasurement (a) on the monthly wage itself or (b) on the number of hours worked in that month. One may also think of young people answering that they are in a regular job when they are only in a youth programme. This is probably true when the programme looks like a regular job – a skilling contract for instance – because young people have signed an employment contract. This contract is specific but it does not always appear so to young people who feel like they are actually working in a regular job. Young people mayalso state that.they are in a regular job because it gives more self esteem. Finally, a tiny proportion of young workers may be temporarily in an illegal situation. Most youth schemes appear in the market sector: Apprenticeship, CQ (Skilling Contract), CA (Adaptation Contract), CO (Orientation Contract) and SIVP (Initiation to Working Life) which disappeared in 1991 and is replaced by CO. One main programme belongs to the non-market sector: TUC (Community Jobs) which became CES (the Solidarity Employment Contract) in 1990.

As Figures 8.3 and 8.4 show, the situation is even worse for young people participating in youth programmes. Even when talking about hourly wage, a huge proportion of young people are below minimum wage. This makes a great deal of sense in France where almost all the youth schemes are regulated so that the wage is a proportion of the SMIC (Table 8.1). When in apprenticeship, young people earn between 15 and 75% of the SMIC according to their age and the length of service in their current job. For the Skilling Contract (CQ), it works the same way but the lower bound is 17%. The Adaptation Contract (CA) pays a fixed proportion of the SMIC (80%) to young people. When in an Orientation Contract, they receive between 30 and 65% of the minimum wage based only on their age. Individuals in Community Work schemes (TUC) – which have been replaced by First Employment schemes – should know that all these regulated amounts are a legal minimum and that the employer may add whatever he wants to this. Solidarity Contracts (CES) are paid at the hourly minimum wage. It should be noted that the latter is a part-time job. Young people in TUC-CES work 20 hours a week and earn approximately 2500 French francs per month. That is the main reason why women appear to be closer to the minimum wage when in youth programmes, since they are mainly in Community work where the hourly wage is exactly the SMIC. Obviously, this does not mean that women earn more than men as Figures 8.3 and 8.4 may suggest. Since they are part-time, women in Community work do earn less than men in market sector programmes on a monthly basis. Finally, the main result remains that the different curves in Figures 8.1 to 8.4 are very close to each other. Even above the minimum wage, low-skilled young French people are not very far from the low wage zone. To this extent, the youth labour market does not show any clear segmentation.

Table 8.1:
Wages in youth schemes

Minimum wages in youth schemes

	Apprent.	CQ	CA	CO	SIVP	TUC-CES
Wage	15% to 75% of the SMIC*	17% to 75% of the SMIC*	80% of the SMIC	30% to 65% of the SMIC	1523.61 to 3149.21*	Hourly SMIC
Conditions	Age and seniority in contract	Age and seniority in contract	Does not vary	Age	Age	Does not vary

Minimum wages in apprenticeship (% of SMIC) from 1988 to 1993[1]

Current duration in the job	Under 18	18–20	21–22	23–28
First semester	15	25	35	45
Second semester	25	35	45	55
Third semester	35	45	55	65
Fourth semester	45	55	65	75
Fifth and sixth semester	60	70	75	75

Minimum wages in skilling contract (CQ) from 1984 onward (% of SMIC)

Current duration in the job	16–17	18	19–25
First semester	17	27	60
Second semester	25	35	65
Third semester	35	45	70
Fourth semester	45	55	75

Initiation to working life in 1990 (in French francs)

	Monthly wage paid by		
Age	Employer	State	Total
Less than 18	1340.61 (26% of the SMIC)	183	1523.61
18–20	1856.21 (36% of the SMIC)	870	2726.21
More than 20	1856.21 (36% of the SMIC)	1293	3149.21

[1] From 1993, the principles remain the same but bounds are moved up (the range has become 25 to 78%)

Wage Equations

The transition from school to work is very often a subject of analysis in France. However, studies are almost always concerned with transition speed or transition rates based on multiple duration models. For instance, specific studies of the wages obtained by young people are rare. The wage issue for young people is nevertheless stressed because we argue that the transition from school to work is closely related to the wage issue since the latter is one of the main variables that characterize a job. The empirical work presented in this section addresses the following question: why do young people start their working life on a low wage?

In order to use a single wage equation to deal with this kind of issue, two assumptions have to be made:

- we first assume that the determinants of young persons' wages are specific and, to some extent, young people are in an earnings regime which is independent from that of employed adults. From an econometric point of view, this justifies the estimation of a single regime equation.

- we also assume that the explanations for low wages are to be found in individual characteristics (training speciality, educational level and diploma, market experience).

In addition, it is also likely that unobserved heterogeneity contributes to the explanation of wage differences, and we control for this by using a variance components model.

Specification and estimation issues.

The data we use come from an unbalanced panel data survey (see Appendix 8.A). It allows us to follow people from June 1989 to February 1995. We use two subsamples according to gender consisting of 971 young men (giving 2664 observations over the whole period), and 808 young women (giving 2230 cases). Our wage equation takes the following form:

$$W_{it} = \mathbf{x}_{it}\,\beta + \alpha_i + u_{it} \qquad (1)$$

where w is the logarithm of the hourly wage expressed in constant prices, α is the individual-specific effect, u is the error term and $\mathbf{x}$ is a vector of explanatory variables containing: training speciality, kind of diploma obtained, type of employment contract, length of time in current job, size of the firm, and previous labour market experience.

• **Selection bias**   We select people having a job at least once in the 5 interview dates from the complete panel data base. One may think about different reasons for not being employed at a given date. The most obvious reasons are: not being interviewed[5], being unemployed or out of the labour force. Other reasons have to do with going through a youth scheme or back to school. Some interviewed people also do declare having a job but do not want to talk about their wage. For all of these reasons, it would be very hard to define a single selection rule for our sample. However, we admit that it may affect the relationship between the dependent variable – the wage here – and the set of explanatory variables. The selection rule would then be 'non-ignorable' for the parameters of interest in our model and so to control for the selection bias, following Nijman and Verbeek (1992), we use three additional variables: 'number of appearances' in the sample, '5 times present' and 'present in the previous sweep'.

• **Independence test of the random individual effect**   One of the main difficulties encountered when estimating the fixed effect model, comes from the fact that the within transformation removes all variables which are constant over time (initial diploma, gender, ...). The corresponding parameters are therefore not identified when the individual effect is treated as fixed. Testing an individual fixed effect model against an individual random effect, in this case, does not make too much sense: all variables remaining constant over time are removed from the set of regressors of both models and that would automatically lead to the non-independence of the random effect. Previous models run on the same population of young people (Balsan *et al.*, 1996) show a strong dependence between the so-called initial human capital variables (which are constant over time) and all the other time varying variables describing the experience in and out of the labour market (number of spells of unemployment and so on).

• **Controlling for heteroscedasticity in an unbalanced panel data set**   In an unbalanced panel data set, the number of appearances in the sample – the number of times the individual is surveyed – varies by individual. It can be shown that, in this case, the variance of the error term depends upon the number of appearances. We are faced with a problem of heteroscedasticity since the variance varies by individual. In the estimated model, this aspect is taken into account by correcting for the heteroscedasticity. First order autocorrelation of the residuals is controlled for as well. It has not been possible to control for higher order autocorrelation since the number of periods available (5) is relatively small.

Results

We now present the results of the wage equation (Table 8.2) where the dependent variable is the hourly wage of young people in constant prices and expressed logarithms. Our aim is to uncover the determinants of wage differences among young persons. As mentioned above, and for obvious reasons, we estimate two separate models by gender.

Table 8.2:

Wage equation: individual random effect model - AR(1)

	Female (N=808; NT=2230)		Male (N=971; NT=2664)	
	Parameter	T	Parameter	t
Intercept	2.6383	14.348	2.9249	14.648
Age	0.69851^E-03	1.463	0.10487^E-02	2.132
Training speciality:				
Tertiary (ref.)				
Industrial	-0.20857^E-01	-1.265	0.21130^E-01	1.416
General	0.29424^E-01	1.100	0.62115^E-01	2.093
Level of diploma:				
No dipl. At all				
(V – Vb) (ref.)				
Bac. with diploma	0.76266^E-01	1.965	0.16834	4.924
Bac. without diploma	0.11889	2.103	0.13406	2.987
BEP / CAP with diploma	0.21437^E-01	0.634	0.47236^E-01	1.604
BEP / CAP without diploma	-0.11866^E-01	-0.334	0.43770^E-01	1.486
Current employment:				
FTC (ref.)				
UDC	-0.15782^E-01	-1.067	0.26949^E-01	1.705
Seniority	-0.87989^E-03	-1.092	0.58837^E-03	0.800
Firm size:				
10–49	0.35317^E-01	2.798	0.30674^E-01	1.958
50–499	0.29923^E-01	2.220	0.82713^E-01	5.050
≥ 500	0.54720^E-01	3.160	0.12496	6.672
Unknown	0.19025^E-01	0.580	0.48784^E-01	1.157
*(Number * duration) of previous spells*:				
1 UDC	-0.10610^E-02	-1.254	-0.89446^E-04	-0.111
≥2 UDC's	-0.36833^E-02	-1.981	0.10503^E-02	0.799
1 precarious job	-0.86807^E-04	-0.094	0.34696^E-03	0.319
≥2 precarious jobs	0.16169^E-03	0.171	-0.12461^E-02	-1.339
1 commercial sector programme	-0.18547^E-02	-1.365	0.22506^E-03	0.152
≥2 commercial sector programmes	-0.47967^E-02	-2.185	-0.19697^E-02	-0.924
1 public programme	-0.17492^E-02	-1.400	-0.51449^E-02	-2.584
≥2 public programmes	-0.68973^E-03	-0.428	-0.27600^E-02	-0.828
1 unemployment spell	-0.45749^E-02	-2.812	-0.56523^E-02	-2.243
≥2 unemployment spells	-0.58793^E-02	-4.755	-0.31423^E-02	-2.204

Table 8.2 (continued)

	Male		Female	
	Parameter	t	Parameter	t
1 spell out of labour force	$0.93773^{E}\text{-}03$	0.253	$0.49835^{E}\text{-}04$	0.011
≥ 2 spells out of labour force	$-0.49737^{E}\text{-}02$	-1.489	$0.33616^{E}\text{-}02$	0.811
Bias variables:				
Number of appearances			$0.23667^{E}\text{-}01$	2.179
Complete presence	$-0.20691^{E}\text{-}01$	-1.089	$-0.11927^{E}\text{-}01$	-0.362
Presence at the previous wave	$-0.28302^{E}\text{-}01$	-1.868	$-0.16240^{E}\text{-}01$	-0.911
Interview Dummy :				
First wave (ref.)				
Second wave	0.68584	3.870	$0.70236^{E}\text{-}01$	0.367
Third wave	0.59630	4.128	$0.80037^{E}\text{-}01$	0.515
Fourth wave	0.63673	4.169	$0.68130^{E}\text{-}01$	0.416
Fifth wave	0.62926	4.068	$0.58612^{E}\text{-}01$	0.355

• **Initial human capital and labour market history**   Our results do not entirely fit with the notion that human capital (initial education, youth training programmes, occupational experience) leads to higher wage. For women and indeed men, having a 'bac' level diploma would significantly lead to a higher wage. From a more general perspective, parameters pertaining to initial human capital are more often statistically significant for males than for females[6]. Conversely, estimated coefficients on labour market history are more significant for women.

For women, one may note the impact of the variables describing the labour market history. Being unemployed or in a market sector youth programme corresponds to the lowest wages. In any case, all these variables have negative coefficients which means that young women experiencing one or several of these situations before entering a job have lower wages than women who have stayed in their job for a long time. One may also note that participation in private sector youth programmes leads to higher wages than a spell of unemployment. However, for a given unemployment duration, having several spells rather than one results in a lower wage. Apparently, queuing on the labour market and searching for a permanent position in the primary sector (Dœringer and Piore, 1971) is more efficient from the wage point of view, rather than going through a series of short duration jobs. For women, losing at least two jobs under unlimited duration contract (UDC) has a negative effect on their subsequent wage. This effect is proportional to the duration of the lost UDC jobs.

In order to understand these results, one has to bear in mind the distinction that has to be made in France between the speed of transition to work and the quality of jobs. Public schemes definitely help young people to make money quickly after leaving school. But they might subsequently stay quite a long time in marginal jobs which are often characterized by low wages. This may also send out bad signals as the duration of unemployment also leads to a lower wage.

For men, training specialities, as one of the main components of the initial education, are important determinants of wage differences. More surprisingly at first sight, a 'general' training speciality, that is to say, having very few vocational skills when entering the labour market, leads to a higher wage. The lack of information on the kind of jobs obtained by those youngsters prevents us from identifying the true mechanism. Nevertheless, one may think of (a) the fact that employers seek general skills rather than specific vocational training they would have to adapt anyway and (b) the same argument as previously: we know that those young people are in the upper part of the wage distribution but we do not know whether all of them did actually get a job. Labour market history leads to lower wages when there are spells of unemployment and community work.

• **The role of firm size, time and selection bias**   A number of other factors are also found to influence wages. The wage increases with the size of the enterprise, whatever the gender. This piece of evidence is not unexpected on the basis of internal labour market theory. An internal market is more likely to be present in the large firms, and this may lead to higher wage and better job stability. For women, the variables indicating the calendar dates give the impression that wages are lower at the first interview with an individual. This is not true for men and the explanation may lie in the fact that most of the young men were doing military service at the date of the first sweep. For both females and males, one of the variables used to test and correct for a selection bias is significant. For women, it is the variable indicating whether she is employed at two successive sweeps: this has a negative impact on the wages. For men, it is the number of appearances in the sample: it has a positive impact on wages.

• **Overqualification and human capital**   The overqualification issue has been increasingly addressed for the last five or ten years. We here mean that young people are overqualified for the job they obtained when they were hired. This could lead to a misunderstanding of the transition from school to work issues and give rise to the misinterpretation of the earning functions. This overqualification would explain the discrepancy between human capital and wage. Because of a mismatch between the required competencies and the young persons' skills, the wage would not be closely linked to the individual initial human capital.

Thus when analysing wage differences in terms of human capital in the case of young people, it is necessary to take account of the match between jobs and skills. If we assume that the return on human capital appears only when this particular human capital is used in the actual production process of the firm, the occupation of pre-'bac'-level young people does not allow them to go further than their job profile permits. In other words, they could go further in terms of initiative, for instance, but the position they occupy does not permit them any autonomy. So, if the wage corresponds to the occupation and not to the individual's human capital, one should observe a weak statistical link between wages and human capital. To some extent, it is what can be observed from our results. All this probably makes sense only in the context of overqualification of hired young people and, to some extent, of all the job applicants.

3   WAGE MOBILITY OF LOW-LEVEL LEAVERS IN FRANCE

Receiving a low wage initially would not be unduly worrying if it means that a young person is able to find work and eventually earn a higher wage. Yet evidence from section 1 (figures 8.1 to 8.4) points to a high degree of stability in the relative wages of young persons. However, this concerns the sample as a whole rather than individual wage mobility, and high overall stability may be the outcome of two opposite moves which cancel each other out. In this section, we take the analysis a step further by examining actual individual wage mobility. We do this in two different ways. First of all, we present cross tabulations of observed wage mobility over the period as a whole and between two successive years. Secondly, we estimate a multinomial Logit model with panel data where the dependent variable indicates upward wage mobility, downward mobility or stability in non-employment. We first provide some stylized facts on cross section occupational status.

The Follow-Up of Young People

The evolution of the experience of young persons in our sample is presented in terms of different types of labour market status. We distinguish between employment with a known wage, and employment where the wage is unknown. The same applies for youth programmes. Since we use the hourly wage, the wage is missing either when the wage itself is missing or when the number of hours worked is missing. We are not able to actually account for the low number of cases for which the hourly wage is known in the first wave. We assume that the interviewed people did not trust us at the time of first interview and above all, we believe that the response rate is highly correlated to the attrition rate. That is to say, the people we do not lose from one interview to another are more willing to answer all the questions, even those regarding the wage.

Figure 8.5
Labour market position – male

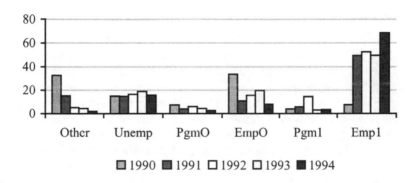

■ 1990 ■ 1991 □ 1992 □ 1993 ■ 1994

Figure 8.6
Labour market position – female

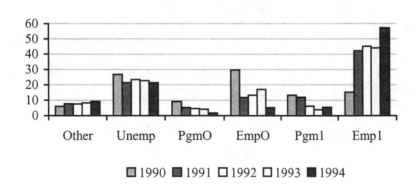

■ 1990 ■ 1991 □ 1992 □ 1993 ■ 1994

pgm0: youth programme with wage unknown; pgm1: youth programme with wage known; emp0: employment with wage unknown; emp1: employment with wage known

Three main labour market states are used: unemployment, on a youth programme and employment. One can see that the proportion of unemployed people remains stable – and even increases for men – during the five years. Obviously (Werquin, 1996) the possibility of entering a youth programme or, for males, the possibility of going to military service ('other' in Figures 8.5 and 8.6) helps considerably to lower the unemployment rate during the early stages of the transition from school to work period. At the same time, employment rises over the period as a whole. The proportion of employed males goes from 50% to almost 80% while the unemployment rate remains constant. The same occurs for women (from 45% to above 60%).

Transitions between the Situations at Different Interviews

Tables 8.3(a) and 8.3(b) show the transitions between waves 4 and 5 of the survey. Tables 8.4(a) and 8.4(b) show the transitions between waves 1 and 5. That is to say the row of each table contains the state at wave t and the column the state at wave t': the figures in the table are the proportions of people being in one state at time t and in an other or the same one at time t'. We thus observe individual transitions in a broad sense because we skip from one interview to another without examining the different states in between. Looking at the same kind of tables month by month would indeed show a much stronger diagonal, but memory bias would be much stronger as well since the monthly information is based on retrospective sections of the questionnaire. In this context, observing mobility between two successive years (Tables 8.3(a) and 8.3(b)) or between the first and the last wave (Tables 8.4(a) and 8.4(b)) allow us to have much more accurate evidence since these are the states of the labour market at the time of the interviews.

From another point of view, two main categories need some explanation. First of all, the survey contains a lot of people having a job without the corresponding hourly wage. Since we did not want to delete these cases, we kept them as people earning a wage with the details of the wage not available (Emp na). Secondly, since a lot of low-skilled young people experience unemployment at the beginning of their working life, this state figures quite often in these transitions. The former, for which the wage is missing in the first sweep, are not concentrated at a particular point of the wage distribution when their wage is available. We thus assume that there is no obvious bias when wage is unobserved.

In Tables 8.3(a) and 8.3(b), between waves 4 and 5 – the end of the observation period – it is clear that as far as jobs are concerned, there is a strong diagonal. That means that, at first sight, individual wage mobility may seem rather poor between these two dates. We know from other computations (not shown) that it is always the case: the diagonal is rather important for two successive sweeps. This leads to two main results. First of all, what we call strong diagonal leaves nevertheless a fair number of individuals going from one fractile of the wage distribution to another: between about one half (females emp5 to emp5) and two thirds (males emp3 to emp3). This means high mobility in a way. Secondly, which really makes us think of a high mobility is the absence of concentration in any of the other cells of the cross tabulation between jobs. To sum up, either young people stay in the same fractile of the wage distribution and exhibit no mobility at all or go to an other fractile of the wage distribution but without any significance about the subsequent status.

Table 8.3(a):

Transitions between wave 4 and wave 5 (%) – female

	Other	Unemp	Pgm na	Emp na	Pgm	Emp1	Emp2	Emp3	Emp4	Emp5	Total
Other	58.9										90
Unemp.	11.2	45.6		14.0	8.0						250
Pgm na		45.7									46
Emp na		12.8	11.2		14.9	10.6	13.3	17.6	17.0		188
Pgm		54.8									42
Emp 1					37.8						98
Emp 2						34.5					87
Emp 3						22.0	35.0				100
Emp 4								35.9	20.4		103
Emp 5									50.5		97
Total											1101

Table 8.3(b):

Transitions between wave 4 and wave 5 (%) – male

	Other	Unemp	Pgm na	Emp na	Pgm	Emp 1	Emp 2	Emp 3	Emp 4	Emp 5	Total
Other											52
Unemp.		44.4				10.3	9.0				223
Pgm na											52
Emp na		8.6	12.1		14.7	13.8	14.2	17.2	16.4		232
Pgm											35
Emp 1					43.9	21.5					130
Emp 2						37.5	21.2				104
Emp 3							30.8	24.8			117
Emp 4								40.2	23.2		112
Emp 5								17.2	59.2		122
Total											1179

Low Pay Among School-Leavers

Legend for Tables 8.3a and 8.3b, 8.4a and 8.4b.

Other	None of the following categories
Unemp	Unemployment
Pgm na	Youth Public Sector Programme (hourly wage not available)
Emp na	Employment (hourly wage not available)
Pgm	Youth Public Sector Programme (with hourly wage available)
Emp1	Bottom of the wage distribution when employed (below decile 20%)
Emp2	Between decile 20% and decile 40% of the wage distribution when employed
Emp3	Between decile 40% and decile 60% of the wage distribution when employed
Emp4	Between decile 60% and decile 80% of the wage distribution when employed
Emp5	Top of the wage distribution when employed (above decile 80%)

Table 8.4(a):
Transitions between waves 1 and 5 (%) – female

	Other	Unemp	Pgm na	Emp na	Pgm	Emp1	Emp 2	Emp 3	Emp 4	Emp 5	Total
Other	26.2	24.6	1.5	4.6	3.1	6.2	9.2	6.2	4.6	13.9	65
Unemp.	17.0	32.0	2.0	6.1	8.2	11.6	5.1	8.8	4.4	14.8	294
Pgm na	6.9	22.8	3.0	3.0	8.9	16.8	10.9	10.9	9.9	6.9	101
Emp na	3.4	13.5	0.6	4.3	2.8	12.2	14.4	13.2	19.3	16.5	327
Pgm	5.5	25.3	2.7	4.1	6.2	14.4	10.3	11.6	8.9	11.0	146
Emp1	0.0	18.2	3.0	15.2	6.1	9.1	18.2	6.1	15.2	9.1	33
Emp2	14.3	7.1	0.0	3.6	3.6	10.7	14.3	39.3	3.6	3.6	28
Emp3	0.0	19.4	0.0	5.6	2.8	19.4	11.1	22.2	11.1	8.3	36
Emp4	2.7	5.4	0.0	5.4	5.4	8.1	10.8	10.8	27.0	24.3	37
Emp5	8.8	11.8	2.9	5.9	2.9	8.8	11.8	5.9	11.8	29.4	34
Total	101	235	18	56	60	135	116	128	126	126	1101

The main evidence can be summarized by three main points:

    - we observe quite a lot of individuals going from unemployment to work;

    - many young people who initially did not declare – or did not know – their wage moved to jobs where they do answer questions about their wages;

    - the transition between one job and another corresponds very often to a shift in the wage: we rarely observe wage stability (transition from a fractile to the same one).

Nevertheless, it is likely that the overall stability of the wages hides a good deal of individual wage mobility. In other words, wages increase for some young people and decrease for others, giving this impression of overall stability. In order to better evaluate the determinants of wage mobility, a multinomial Logit model is now estimated.

Table 8.4(b):

Transitions between waves 1 and 5 (%) – male

	Other	Unemp	Pgm na	Emp na	Pgm	Emp1	Emp2	Emp3	Emp4	Emp5	Total
Other	1.8	12.5	2.3	8.3	3.9	15.1	14.3	15.6	12.5	13.5	384
Unemp.	3.4	25.6	4.0	7.4	6.3	17.6	12.5	8.5	7.4	7.4	176
Pgm na	2.3	33.0	2.3	6.8	6.8	10.2	12.5	10.2	9.1	6.8	88
Emp na	1.3	11.1	1.8	8.1	1.0	11.9	15.4	12.4	19.2	17.7	395
Pgm	2.1	23.4	4.3	10.7	10.6	14.9	8.5	6.4	6.4	12.8	47
Emp 1	0.0	11.8	17.7	0.0	0.0	17.7	11.8	11.8	29.4	0.0	17
Emp 2	0.0	17.7	0.0	17.7	0.0	17.7	0.0	29.4	11.8	5.9	17
Emp 3	5.3	0.0	0.0	5.3	0.0	5.3	31.6	10.5	26.3	15.8	19
Emp 4	0.0	5.6	0.0	0.0	0.0	0.0	11.1	33.3	33.3	16.8	18
Emp 5	0.0	11.1	5.6	5.6	0.0	16.7	5.6	0.0	11.1	44.4	18
Total	22	185	31	93	41	162	164	151	168	162	1179

Explanation: For instance, between waves 1 and 5, 17.7% of the 20% people at the bottom of the wage distribution (Emp1) remain at the bottom of the wage distribution (Emp1). During the same period, 11.8% of the 20% people at the bottom of the wage distribution (Emp1) move to the next group: those earning a wage between the second and the fourth decile (Emp2).

A Multinomial Logit Analysis of Individual Wage Mobility

A fixed effect multinomial Logit model is estimated with the following dependent variable:

- its value is 2 when, between two successive interviews, we observe an improvement in the wage of the individual. This could be achieved through an upward movement in the wage distribution – from one fractile to a higher one – or though a move from non-employment (unemployment or out of the labour force) to employment;

- its value is 1 when the individual remains in a similar situation – in the same portion of the wage distribution – or when we observe a worsening of his/her wage situation. That could be through a downward movement in the wage distribution - from one fractile to a lower one – or through a move from

employment to non – employment (unemployment or out of the labour force).
- its value is 0 when the individual is not employed at both dates. All coefficients are interpreted relative to the latter status.

Table 8.5
Determinants of wage mobility – females

Variable (at least one spell experienced)	Downward mobility Coefficient	Std. error	Upward mobility Coefficient	Std. error
1 UDC	-2.7446	0.3349	-1.7055	0.3152
≥2 UDCs	-3.3094	0.7328	-2.5183	0.7510
1 precarious job	*-0.0908	0.2591	-0.3305	0.2301
≥2 precarious jobs	-0.8640	0.3878	-1.1394	0.3504
1 market sector programme	2.9189	0.4433	1.1124	0.2804
≥2 market sector programmes	5.3662	0.8344	1.3320	0.5366
≥1 public programmes	3.2067	0.5098	1.7996	0.3516
1 unemployment spell	2.4219	0.3652	0.9985	0.2728
≥2 unemployment spells	4.3194	0.4978	2.0328	0.3840
≥1 spell out of the labour force	0.9573	0.5644	*0.4265	0.4370

*: not significant at 5% level

Table 8.6:
Determinants of wage mobility – males

Variable (a least one spell experienced)	Downward mobility Coefficient	Std. error	Upward mobility Coefficient	Std. error
1 UDC	-0.8169	0.2374	*-0.2299	0.2158
≥2 UDCs	-2.1732	0.4783	-1.1284	0.4334
1 precarious job	*0.3111	0.2357	*-0.1777	0.1983
≥2 precarious jobs	*0.4973	0.3178	*-0.3420	0.2706
1 market sector programme	1.7172	0.3131	0.7403	0.2441
≥2 market sector programmes	3.4048	0.7541	2.3056	0.6159
≥1 public programmes	2.1545	0.6819	0.9853	0.4403
1 unemployment spell	2.1222	0.2887	0.9893	0.2230
≥2 unemployment spells	3.3284	0.3748	1.7386	0.2904
≥1 spell out of the labour force	*0.7857	0.5188	*0.2459	0.4492

The estimation method does not allow for the use of time constant explanatory variables. Thus Tables 8.5 and 8.6 contain the parameters of the variables describing the individual labour market history in the explanation of the quality of the wage mobility.

Having lost one or more unlimited duration contract (UDC) corresponds to a lower probability of an improvement or a worsening in the wage situation. (The probability of staying unemployed or out of the labour force is thus increased.) The decrease in probability is, nevertheless, less pronounced for the upward mobility category (i.e. an improvement in the wage). For young females, having had at least two jobs with fixed-term contracts (FTC) decreases the probability of a worsening of the wage situation. But, having experienced one or more FTC also decreases the probability of an improvement. The overall effect of FTCs is negative.

For young males, the impact of FTCs is not significant at a 10% level as far as upward mobility is concerned. On the other hand, the impact of FTCs on downward mobility is positive but not very significant in statistical terms. This means that having experienced FTC increases the probability of downward mobility. Market sector youth schemes have a positive impact on both the probability of a worsening of the individual wage situation and the probability of an improvement. This effect remains but is weaker for the non market sector youth programmes. One may note that these positive effects are higher for the probability of a worsening. It seems though that having participated in youth schemes helps young people in avoiding non-employment (unemployment or out of the labour force). This confirms that the role of these youth programmes is more to help young people in finding a job rather than in increasing their human capital (which is normally associated with a higher wage). Past unemployment also has a positive effect which appears to be in between the two kinds of youth scheme; there is an exception though for males and for the probability of an improvement in the wage situation where past unemployment has the highest effect. In conclusion, this model shows the complex role of the variables describing the labour market history of young people: losing a UDC has a negative effect, the role of the FTC is unclear. Youth schemes seem to permit better access to jobs, but not to higher wages.

4   CONCLUSIONS

Our approach has been essentially empirical and must be viewed as a first attempt to figure out how wage mobility works in France at the beginning of the 90s even if the focus of the paper is central to policy makers – one of the keywords in France currently is wage flexibility. Indeed, it is now very often assumed that employers require a lowering of the minimum wage in order to hire young people. But it is also very often argued that the minimum wage threshold does not exist any more for young people given the dramatic increase in the use of temporary contracts or other youth schemes.

There are very few theories that describe the issues we deal with. As an example, our approach could be criticized according to the dualist theory since we do not model transitions between internal and external market jobs. The dualist theory thus would allocate all those youngsters in the panel to the secondary segment of the labour market: statistical inference with a single wage equation would then be uninteresting. However, estimating a single wage equation helps us in two different ways:

- it is a starting point for analysing the specificities of wage formation in the youth labour market;

- it is also a way to figure out whether, among the education/training levels of those early school-leavers, some are more relevant than others in explaining wage differences.

On the other hand, one may think of bad labour market history in explaining a low wage. Matching theory (Jovanovic, 1979) explains that high productivity at work comes from a good match between wage earner and job. In the face of the ongoing overqualification of hired young people, it is therefore likely that jobs once associated with low skills now require higher skills. At least, people with higher levels of diploma than before are now applying for that kind of so-called low-skilled job. In this case, the wage would be a function of individual characteristics and of the gap between the qualification level required and that supplied by the applicant, for the job. This leads to a more complex statistical specification than that presented here and is the subject of ongoing research.

APPENDIX 8.A: THE DATA

The data we analyse were collected by the French Research Centre for Education, Training and Employment (CEREQ), a public research centre in France which undertakes studies and surveys of the relationship between education, training, work and employment. One of its divisions is the School to Working Life Transition Department (DEVA) which is a national observatory that provides detailed analyses of training and degree specializations and of transitions from school to working life; identifies the mechanisms through which these transitions occur, and studies the potential competition between certain kinds of training. The aim of these studies is to understand the relations between training and employment and between recruitment within the working population and that of young people leaving the educational system. This data source is a panel data survey based on five interviews which take place annually during a six-year period - from January 1989 to January 1995, after the individual has left the educational system in June 1989, and a bit before to allow for the observation of early leaving during the academic year (from September to June as a general rule). The survey we use is actually the second CEREQ telephone panel data survey. It follows young people who left school or a Centre for apprenticeship in 1989. About two thousand three hundred people (2333) were then interviewed in December 1990, 1991, 1992, 1993 and in January 1995. The average age of the surveyed individual was about 18 in 1989. Such a survey allows the study of various labour market itineraries: participation in youth programmes, sequences of jobs occupied according to their status, qualification, vocational speciality, movement between employment, unemployment and out of the labour force. All jobs that take place in this six-year period are known and, of course, details of the corresponding wages are also requested from those interviewed. They actually do answer quite readily to all sorts of resources questions. Table 8.A.1 summarizes the characteristics of the male and female samples. The data also indicate that the mean of the number of jobs occupied was about 2.18, that women had slightly more marginal jobs and far fewer regular jobs than men, that some of these young people had more than five jobs during the period and that 20% of the individuals were constantly jobless.

Table 8.A.1

Descriptive statistics

	Females		Males		Definitions
	Mean	St. err	Mean	St. err	of variables
Age (in years)	22.25	2.03	22.3	2.12	Age of the person at the time of the survey
Training speciality:					**Vocational background, if any**
Tertiary (ref.)	0.5587	0.4966	0.2575	0.4373	Tertiary
Industrial	0.2638	0.4407	0.5559	0.4969	Industrial
General	0.1776	0.3822	0.1866	0.3896	Little vocational background (early leaving or general bac level)

Table 8.A.1 (continued)

	Females		Males		Definition
	Mean	St. err	Mean	St. err	of variables
Level – Diploma:					**Cross variable: diploma and educational level**
No dipl. at all (V or Vb) (ref.)	0.1371	0.3440	0.1884	0.3910	No diploma at all (early leaving mainly)
Bac. with diploma	0.1516	0.3587	0.1944	0.3956	Bac* level with the bac* diploma
Bac. without diploma	0.0218	0.1461	0.0360	0.1862	Reaching bac level but exam not taken
BEP / CAP with diploma	0.5057	0.5000	0.3761	0.4845	First French vocational diploma
BEP / CAP without diploma	0.1838	0.3874	0.2051	0.4034	First French vocational level (no diploma)
Current employment:					**Description of the current job**
UDC (ref. FTC)	0.7870	0.4094	0.7988	0.1607	The current employment is an unlimited duration contract
Seniority	25.3157	16.5541	24.4373	15.2908	Duration in the current job
Firm size : 10–49	0.2731	0.4456	0.2812	0.4496	The enterprise has between 10 and 49 employees
Firm size : 50–499	0.2978	0.4574	0.3014	0.4590	The enterprise has between 50 and 499 employees
Firm size > 500	0.1049	0.3065	0.1809	0.3850	The enterprise has more than 500 employees
Firm size : unknown	0.0152	0.1226	0.0176	0.1317	The individual does not know the size of his firm
Number of previous spells (Tables 6 and 7):					**Labour market history**
1 UDC	0.1483	0.3554	0.2151	0.4038	One unlimited duration contract in the past
≥2 UDCs	0.0216	0.1454	0.0340	0.1823	Two or more unlimited duration contracts in the past
1 precarious job	0.3493	0.4768	0.3646	0.4814	One precarious job in the past
≥2 precarious jobs	0.2195	0.414	0.2686	0.4433	Two or more precarious jobs in the past
1 private sector programme	0.2019	0.4014	0.1876	0.3904	One private sector youth programme in the past

Table 8.A.1 (continued)

	Females		Males		Definition
	Mean	St. err	Mean	St. err	of variables
≥2 private sector programmes	0.0559	0.2297	0.0521	0.2222	Two or more private sector programmes in the past
1 public sector programme	0.2372	0.4254	0.1022	0.3030	One spell of 'community work' in the past
≥2 public sector programmes	0.0611	0.2395	0.0155	0.1237	Two or more spells of 'community work' in the past
1 unemployment spell	0.3485	0.4765	0.2842	0.4511	One unemployment spell in the past
≥2 unemployment spells	0.3327	0.4712	0.2830	0.4505	Two or more unemployment spells in the past
1 spell out of the labour force	0.3643	0.4813	0.3815	0.4858	One spell of inactivity in the past
≥2 spells out of the labour force	0.0744	0.2624	0.0805	0.2720	Two or more spells of inactivity in the past

Number × duration of previous spells (wage equation – Table 1):

	Females		Males		Definition
1 UDC	1.7291	5.3735	2.9489	6.6333	One Unlimited Duration Contract in the past
≥2 UDCs	0.4009	2.9370	0.6674	3.7680	Two or more Unlimited Duration Contracts in the past
1 precarious job	4.2538	7.6152	3.3288	6.1030	One precarious job in the past
≥2 precarious jobs	4.0628	8.2991	4.8491	8.8275	Two or more precarious jobs in the past
1 private sector programme	2.2143	5.9453	1.6543	4.8789	One private sector youth programme in the past
≥2 private sector programme	0.5538	3.4594	0.4309	3.0704	Two or more private sector programmes in the past
1 public sector programme	2.7426	6.8226	0.7207	3.5802	One spell of 'community work' in the past
≥2 public sector programmes	0.8865	4.8002	0.1126	1.7055	Two or more spells of 'community works' in the past
1 unemployment spell	2.0596	4.5523	1.0161	2.5749	One unemployment spell in the past

Table 8.A.1 (continued)

	Females		Males		Definitions
	Mean	st. err	Mean	st. err	of variables
≥2 unemployment spells	3.8839	7.4734	2.5435	5.7593	Two or more unemployment spells in the past
1 spell out of the labour force	0.9386	2.2284	0.8589	1.4964	One spell of inactivity in the past
≥2 spells out of the labour force	0.3785	2.0385	0.3071	1.4974	Two or more spells of inactivity in the past
Bias variables:					**Control for bias**
Number of appearances	3.4726	1.2219	3.3011	1.0537	Number of times the individual is present in the panel
Complete presence	0.1928	0.3946	0.0638	0.2445	Five appearances (present in all waves)
Presence in the previous wave	05825	0.4933	0.5619	0.4962	Present the year before in the panel (previous wave)

* The bac is one of the main French diplomas: it gives the right to go to university and is usually taken at 18.

NOTES

1   See *Économie et Statistique* (1995 and 1997) for a collection of articles addressing the French case.
2   Vero and Werquin, 1998
3   This French diploma is the one which allows young people to enter university.
4   One may note that we use hourly wage controlled for the price index.
5   The attrition rate is about 20% per year.
6   These results are confirmed by the estimation of a random effect Probit model where the dependent variable takes the value 1 when the young people belong to the fraction of the population that has a wage above the decile 40%.

REFERENCES

Balsan, D., Hanchane, S. and Werquin, P. (1996), 'Mobilité professionnelle initiale : éducation et expérience sur le marché du travail', *Economie et Statistique*, **229**, 91–106.

Baltagi, B.H. (1995), *Econometric Analysis of Panel Data*, Wiley.

Dœringer, P. and Piore, M. (1971), *Internal Labour Market and Manpower Analysi*s, Lexington, Massachusetts.

Guillotin, Y. and Sevestre, P. (1994), 'Estimations de fonctions de gains sur données de panel : endogénéité du capital humain et effets de la sélection', *Economie et Prévision*, **116**, 119–135.

Hausman, J.A. (1978), 'Specification tests in econometrics', *Econometrica*, **46**, 1251-1271.

Hsiao, C. (1992), 'Logit and Probit Models', in Mátyás, L. and P. Sevestre (eds.), *The Econometrics of Panel Data - Handbook of Theory and Applications*, Kluwer Academic Publishers.

Jovanovic, B. (1979), 'Job Matching and the Theory of Turnover', *Journal of Political Economy*, **5**, 972–990.

Nijman, T. and Verbeek, M. (1992), 'Testing for selectivity bias in panel data models', *International Economic Review*, **3**, 681–703.

Vero and Werquin (1998)

Werquin, P. (1996), 'De l'école à l'emploi, les parcours précaires', dans S. Paugam (ed.) *L'exclusion : l'état des savoirs*, Paris: Editions La Découverte.

Werquin, P. (1997), 'Dix ans d'intervention sur le marché du travail des jeunes en France, 1986-1996', *Économie et Statistique*, **304**, 121–306.

9. Low Wages of School-Leavers of Vocational Education in the Netherlands

Wendy Smits and Ed Willems

---

1   INTRODUCTION

In most western economies there is an substantial inequality between individuals' incomes. Some people earn more than others, even if their qualifications seem to be the same. In this chapter we examine wage differences between people with the same educational background. Educational background, together with years of work experience, is a very important factor in explaining wage differences between individuals. Nevertheless, wage differences between people with the same educational background and work exprience can be considerable. One of the reasons for this might be that not all people have an occupation that matches their educational background. People that have jobs that do not match their educational background cannot use all the skills they possess and as a result will have lower earnings. Furthermore, if the situation endures, they might be confronted by skill obsolescence, which will prevent them from switching to an occupation that better matches their educational background.

Mismatches between education and the labour market are most manifest among school-leavers.[1] Not all school-leavers will immediately succeed in finding a job that matches their educational qualifications. This may be a result of a lack of transparency in the labour market. In that case it is to be expected that it will take some time before a good match is reached. School-leavers first try different kind of jobs and finally end up in a job that gives a good match with their skills and abilities. With respect to this Hirschleifer (1973) makes a distinction between jobs as 'inspection goods' and jobs as 'experience goods.' Mismatches may, however, also be caused by shifts in demands and supply for a type of education. School leavers have to accept an occupation that does not match their educational background because due to a fall in demand there are not sufficient jobs that match their own type of education. In that case, mismatches will very often not be temporary, because at the time that demand for their type of education increases again, people

177

able to switch because of skill obsolescence.

In this chapter we will focus on wages of school-leavers from secondary vocational education in the Netherlands. We will examine the extent to which low wages of school-leavers are caused by mismatches between educational background and occupation. The structure of this chapter is as follows. First, we discuss some theories on the relation between education, occupation and earnings. Subsequently, we briefly discuss the human capital theory, the labour queue theory and the theory of job matching. These theories provide several alternative explanations for differences of wages and especially the role of education in this. Section 3 gives an empirical overview of the wage distribution of school-leavers of secondary vocational education in the Netherlands. In section 4, we estimate earnings equations to identify the most important explanatory factors for differences in wages. We then go on to analyse the probability of earning a low wage.

2   THEORIES ON EARNINGS

The difference in earnings between individuals or nations has been of interest for economists for many years. In this section we will focus on the role of education in economic theory on earnings. The neo-classical, *human capital theory* (Schultz, 1961; Becker, 1962) explains the individual's wage differentials by the differences in human capital acquired, which causes the productivity of individuals to differ. The central element of this theory is that – analogously to firms' investments in physical capital – individuals invest in their human capital in order to become more productive in jobs. In general, the investments in education are regarded as the most important, but one can also invest in health, geographical mobility, etc.. It is assumed that people who are higher educated or more experienced, i.e. who have received more on-the-job training, are more productive in all jobs. As in this neo-classical context workers are rewarded according to their marginal productivity, higher educated workers earn more then less educated workers.

Human capital theory assumes that individuals have perfect information on the future labour market. In general this will not be the case, however. Education will take time, and during that time the labour market may change. The individual will therefore not be certain on the returns to his investments in education. Due to a decrease in the demand for his type of education the return might be less than expected. According to the human capital theory, market forces ensure that this decrease in returns will be the same for all individuals with the same educational background. Human capital theory does therefore not explain wage differences between people with the same educational background, in as far as these differences are not a result of differences in personal characteristics.

In contrast to the assumption in human capital theory that the individual's wage depends on personal skills and capabilities only, the *labour queue theory* developed by Thurow (1979) states that wages are completely determined by job characteristics. Each job has its specific character, and productivity in that job is solely determined by job characteristics. This means that the job concerned is the only relevant factor in explaining the wage and the individual's abilities play no role.

This different concept does not imply that educational background is not important within the labour queue context. The basic idea of this theory is that in order to fulfil a job, specific knowledge and skills, that can only be acquired by means of on-the-job training and not by initial schooling, are required. As this on-the-job training involves costs, employers will rank all individuals according to their expected training costs (the labour queue): workers with the lowest expected training costs will be employed first. In general it is assumed that people with a higher educational level are easier to train than people with a lower level of education. Therefore their position in the labour queue will be in favour of those who are less educated. So a higher educational background increases the chance of being employed in a well paid job, according to this theory, but there will be no wage differences between people working in the same job but having a different edcuational background.

The theory of job matching can be seen as a synthesis of the *labour queue* and *human capital theories*. It is argued that personal abilities and job characteristics both determine the individual's earnings (see for example Hartog, 1992). Productivity in a job depends on the match between personal characteristics and job characteristics. As a consequence an individual's earnings are highest in jobs that give a good match with their personal characteristics. Given their individual characteristics, like educational background, people have a *comparative advantage* in specific jobs.[2]

Most matching models focus on the match between someone's educational level and the job level (see e.g. Hartog and Oosterbeek, 1988; Cohn and Kahn, 1995). The return to schooling will be highest if the match is perfect, *i.e.* if the job level equals the educational level one has obtained. However, this approach excludes the role of the branch of study. Arguing along the lines of the job matching theory it can be stated that the individual's productivity and thus the returns to schooling will be highest if he or she is working in the area their studies refer to, so people with technical education in the technical occupations, people with economic education in economic professions, etc.. So, following the job matching theory, people that have a job that does not match either their level of education or branch of education will have lower earnings[3] because not all skills they have acquired during their study can be made productive.

The *labour queue* and the *job matching theory* can both provide satisfactory explanations of wage differentials between people with the same educational background. Both theories predict that job characteristics cause wage differentials between persons with the same educational background.The main difference between the theories is that according to the *labour queue theory* educational background does not matter for earnings while according to the *job matching theory* it is the match between educational background and job characteristics that determines individual earnings.

3   WAGE DISTRIBUTION FOR SCHOOL-LEAVERS IN THE NETHERLANDS

In this section we will have an initial look at the wage distribution of Dutch school-leavers from full-time secondary vocational education. Full-time secondary vocational education consists of two phases; preparatory and intermediate education. Preparatory Vocational Education (PVE) is a four-year programme that prepares pupils for Intermediate Vocational Education or an apprenticeship scheme. Within Intermediate Vocational Education (IVE) we can distinguish two variants, a short variant (2 or 3-year programme) and a long variant (4-year programme). We will distinguish four educational branches: *agriculture, technical, economics and business administration* and *community care* (for example nursing professions).

Information on school-leavers is available from the RUBS[4]-survey. This is a large scale annual survey among school-leavers from, amongst others, Preparatory and Intermediate Vocational Education, some 9 months after they have completed their courses (see Van Smoorenburg and Willems, 1996). Information in the survey includes the current labour market position of the school-leaver, the occupational requirements of the job the school-leaver is working in, the sector of industry, gross hourly wages and several other background variables.

Table 9.1 gives the wage distribution of school-leavers by age, gender, and ethnic background. Since age of the school-leaver and educational level are closely related, the variation in age is very small between school-leavers of a given educational level. Therefore differences between different age groups are probably to a large extent caused by differences in educational background. The wage distribution of school-leavers of 16 or 17 years old, only overlaps the wage distribution of school-leavers older than 21 in the upper decile of its distribution. Besides, the standard deviation is somewhat higher for the older age categories.

Table 9.1:

Gross hourly earnings in guilders of school-leavers by age, gender, and ethnic group

	Mean	Std.dev	Lowest decile	Lower quartile	Median	Upper quartile	Highest decile
Age:							
16–17	6.48	2.62	3.64	4.93	6.02	7.69	9.74
18–19	8.22	3.40	5.27	6.31	7.57	9.66	11.54
20–21	11.42	3.70	7.67	9.05	10.87	13.36	15.59
>21	14.42	4.20	10.38	11.73	14.03	16.18	19.21
Sex:							
Male	10.56	4.98	5.19	6.87	9.78	13.85	16.73
Female	10.58	4.21	5.77	7.69	10.15	13.10	15.58
Ethnic background:							
Dutch	10.56	4.63	5.43	7.21	10.02	13.34	16.15
Other	10.88	4.06	6.20	8.17	10.77	12.98	16.44
Total	**10.57**	**4.62**	**5.43**	**7.21**	**10.06**	**13.34**	**16.15**

Source: ROA: RUBS 1995

Furthermore, the table shows that on average women do not earn less than men. The variation in earnings is somewhat higher for men than women. Surprisingly, members of ethnic minorities on average earn more than native school-leavers. This may be because these school-leavers are on average older than Dutch school-leavers, and so they automatically earn more because of the legal minimum wage.

As stated above, wage differentials may to a great extent be the result of differences in educational level acquired, and this is shown in Table 9.2. Gross hourly earnings rise sharply with educational level. Also, the variation in wages increases with the level. This is probably a result of the minimum wage legislation that has much more influence on the wage distribution of school-leavers from Preparatory Vocational Education than on the distribution of wages of school-leavers from Intermediate and short Intermediate Vocational Education. However, the branch of study is also relevant. The average hourly wages of school-leavers from agriculture, economics and community care do not vary much. The median income is, however, somewhat higher for school-leavers from community care education. School-leavers with a technical background earn on average less than others. However, this may be partly caused by the overrepresentation of technical studies within the PVE level. The variation in hourly wages of school-leavers with a technical background is larger. Remarkably, the variation in wages of school-leavers from economics and business administration is relatively small.

Table 9.2:

Gross hourly earnings in guilders of school-leavers
by educational level and educational branch group

	Mean	Std.dev	Lowest decile	Lower quartile	Median	Upper quartile	Highest decile
Educational level:							
PVE	6.97	2.76	3.89	5.27	6.49	8.50	10.38
Short IVE	9.69	3.64	6.09	7.29	8.92	11.54	14.23
IVE	12.71	4.36	7.98	9.81	12.40	15.00	17.31
Educational branch:							
Agriculture	10.80	4.58	5.77	7.29	10.30	13.85	16.73
Technics	10.29	4.95	4.96	6.49	9.38	13.64	16.44
Economics	10.79	4.03	6.35	8.08	10.38	12.98	15.58
Community							
Care	10.91	4.80	5.32	7.44	10.69	13.56	16.15

PVE = Preparatory Vocational Education
IVE = Intermediate Vocational Education
Source: ROA: RUBS 1995

We now take a closer look at the group of school-leavers that earn a 'low wage'. A low wage is defined as a gross hourly wage that is less than two-thirds of the median gross hourly wage of the educational category. An educational category is defined by branch and level, for example 'technical preparatory vocational education'. A low wage is always defined relative to the educational category someone belongs to. The rationale for this is that individuals that considers to invest in a certain type of education, will look at the earnings distribution of people that have completed this type of education, in order to get an idea of the expected returns of their investment. If their actual earnings after completing their education are much lower than median earnings for the whole category then their investment has not yielded the expected returns.[5]

Table 9.3 gives the proportion of school-leavers that earn a low wage by educational category. The risk of ending up with a low wage for school-leavers from technical and economic vocational education is highest for those who only completed Preparatory Vocational Education. Among school-leavers from agricultural or community care education the risk of a low wage is on the contrary highest for those that have attended Intermediate Vocational Education. Remarkably, for school-leavers from economics and business administration type of education the risk is fairly low for all educational levels, which is in line with the relatively low variance in earnings for this branch of study.

Table 9.3:
Percentage of school-leavers that earn a relatively low wage

	PVE	Short-IVE	IVE	Total
Agriculture	10	2	15	13
Technical	13	10	10	12
Economics	9	6	6	6
Community care	6	6	14	12
Total	**12**	**8**	**10**	**10**

Source: ROA: RUBS 1995

Table 9.4:
Percentage of school-leavers that earn a low wage
by (mis)match with respect to level

	Job level matches educational level	Job level below educational level
PVE	10	15
Short IVE	8	8
IVE	5	17
Total	7	**15**

Source: ROA: RUBS 1995

We expect to find a close relation between low wages and mismatches between education and occupation. Table 9.4 gives the proportion of school-leavers that earn a low wage for school-leavers who are working in a job that requires less education than they have actually obtained and school-leavers working in a job that exactly matches their level of education. About 15% of the school-leavers experiencing a mismatch with respect to level earn a low wage. For those who experience no mismatch, the proportion of low wage earners is only half as large (7%). For mismatches with respect to branch of study the difference is not that large, as Table 9.5 shows. Of those who experience a mismatch with respect to branch 11% earn a low wage, for those who experience no mismatch this is 8%. Remarkably, for school-leavers from Preparatory Vocational Education a mismatch with respect to branch even seems to reduce the risk of a 'low wage'.

Table 9.5:
Percentage of school-leavers that earn a low wage
by (mis)match with respect to branch

	Job branch matches educational branch	Job branch does not match educational branch
PVE	15	8
Short IVE	8	7
IVE	5	14
Total	**8**	**11**

Source: ROA: RUBS 1995

4   EXPLAINING WAGE DIFFERENCES OF SCHOOL-LEAVERS

In the previous section we saw that in general mismatches increase the probability of a low wage, but are certainly not the only factor explaining the low wages of some school-leavers, since not everyone who experiences a mismatch also earns a low wage. In this section we will have a closer look at factors that influence wages of school-leavers. We first estimate wage equations for school-leavers before going on to analyse the probability of receiving a low wage.

Apart from the theoretically derived variables on educational background (both educational level and branch) and job characteristics (job level and branch), wages are thought to depend on organizational characteristics and personal characteristics too. Separate wage equations will be estimated for different branches of studies. This is done because the returns to years of education within a specific branch of study can also depend on the supply and demand ratio for that branch. For example, if the supply of labour within a specific branch and level increases, wages could fall at that level and the returns to education will decrease. Table 9.6 gives the regression results.

Not unexpectedly, wages of school-leavers increase significantly with age. The age–earnings profile of school-leavers of economic and administrative vocational education is, however, much steeper than for the other branches. The influence of age on earnings may reflect the influence of experience or it may be a result of minimum wage legislation; in the Netherlands the minimum wage increases with age until the age of 23. Since the variation in experience between school-leavers is very low the latter is more likely than the former.

Once a correction is made for other factors influencing wages women do earn less than men in all branches. The wage difference is not significant, however, for school-leavers from community care vocational education. This might be because school-leavers from this branch of education are nearly all women. The largest wage difference between males and females is found among school-leavers of agricultural vocational education. Corrected for the other factors included in the analysis, women earn about 19% less than men. Part of this wage difference may be caused by differences in specialization. Van Smoorenburg and Willems (1996), for instance, show that the specializations most popular with women ('flower arrangement' and 'animal care') have the lowest wages on average.

Most important in the context of this study are the variables that refer to educational and occupational characteristics. The level of education is specified in years. The appendix to this chapter gives the number of years for each level of education. The actual years of schooling of a school-leaver can be split into the number of years of schooling that is required for the job he is working in and the number of years of over- or underschooling. Overschooling and underschooling are defined as the difference between the number of years that someone has studied and the number of years that is required for the job. Overschooling refers to a higher educational level than required, whereas underschooling implies that an individual has had less schooling than the job requires.[6]

If the returns to overschooling and underschooling were zero, it is the job level that matters in determining wages and not the educational level. The *labour queue theory* therefore predicts zero coefficients for years of over- and underschooling. If on the other hand the coefficients of years of overschooling and underschooling in the equation were equal to the coefficients of the number of years of schooling required for the job then it is the actual level of schooling of the school-leaver, that matters for earnings instead of the job level, as the *human capital theory* predicts. In that case people that are working in a job on a lower level than their educational level will not earn less than they would have earned in a job that matches their educational level. According to the *job matching theory* it is expected that the

Table 9.6:

Wage equations by branch of study (absolute t-values in brackets)

	Agriculture	Technical	Economics	Community care
Schooling required:				
For job (years)	0.075	0.087	0.024	0.141
	**(2.75)	**(5.03)	(1.36)	**(7.83)
Match:				
Overschooling	0.072	0.056	0.011	0.099
(years)	**(2.62)	**(3.14)	(0.58)	**(5.41)
Underschooling	-0.099	-0.081	-0.054	-0.112
(years)	**(2.04)	**(2.76)	*(1.71)	**(3.40)
Mismatch by	-0.043	-0.036	-0.039	-0.127
branch	(1.16)	(1.59)	**(2.20)	**(4.90)
Undertaking	-0.017	-0.026	-0.049	-0.199
apprenticeship	(0.29)	(0.85)	(0.89)	**(5.93)
Personal characteristics:				
Age	0.231	0.261	0.481	0.120
	**(2.77)	**(4.69)	**(5.50)	**(4.85)
Age squared	-0.003	-0.004	-0.009	-0.002
	*(1.86)	**(3.38)	**(4.25)	**(4.07)
Female	-0.186	-0.054	-0.077	0.020
	**(5.70)	**(2.21)	**(4.25)	(0.38)
Ethnic minority	0.223	-0.114	-0.070	0.085
	(0.65)	**(1.91)	(1.56)	(1.32)
Organizational characteristics:				
Firm size				
< 10 workers	Reference	Reference	Reference	Reference
10–99 workers	0.049	0.028	0.023	-0.002
	(1.40)	(1.09)	(1.02)	(0.08)
100–499 workers	0.112	0.052	0.074	0.074
	*(1.96)	(1.53)	**(2.53)	**(1.99)
>500 workers	0.113	0.082	0.046	-0.009
	*(2.05)	**(2.55)	*(1.87)	(0.25)
Profit organization	-0.002	-0.004	-0.073	-0.088
	(0.05)	(0.12)	**(2.65)	**(3.29)
Constant	-1.832	-2.265	-3.936	-0.945
	**(2.27)	**(4.32)	**(4.64)	**(3.37)
Adjusted R^2	0.35	0.51	0.35	0.41
	$F_{(13,472)}=$	$F_{(13,935)}=$	$F_{(13,1129)}=$	$F_{(15,937)}=$
	21.10^{**}	76.52^{**}	48.71^{**}	51.76^{**}

* significant at 10%-level; ** significant at 5%-level

coefficients on years of over- and underschooling will be greater than zero but smaller than coefficients of years of schooling required. People who are working in a job that requires less education than is actually acquired, will earn less than those with the same educational background working in a job that matches their education but more than those working in the same job but having less education.

The number of years of schooling required for the job has the biggest impact on wages of school-leavers from community care vocational education. For school-leavers of agricultural and technical vocational education the impact of the required level is much smaller. For economic vocational education the coefficient on the number of years of schooling required is not even significantly different from zero.

Overschooling does not have a significant impact on wages of school-leavers from economics and business administration vocational education. Since the number of years required for the job has no significant impact on wages either, this result is difficult to interpret, because it means that neither the job level nor the educational level of the school-leaver has any impact on wages. However, the (negative) return of underschooling is significant at the 10%-level as can be seen from Table 9.6. For the other branches the hypothesis of zero coefficients is rejected at the 5% level.

The hypothesis that the return to overschooling is equal to the return of the number of required years of schooling is not rejected for agricultural vocational education. So, school-leavers from agricultural vocational education do not earn significantly less if they are working in a job below their educational level. On the other hand, if they are working in a job which requires a higher level of education they will earn less than what they would have earned in a job that matches their educational level. School-leavers from technical and community care vocational education earn less in jobs that require less education than they actually have acquired than in jobs that match their actual educational level but the returns to years of overschooling are nevertheless positive. Their earnings in a job that requires a higher level of education than they actually have are not significantly different from earnings in jobs that match their level of education.

Furthermore, we included a dummy variable for a mismatch with respect to branch of study. From Table 9.6 it follows that a mismatch between branch of study and occupation only leads to lower earnings for school-leavers from economic vocational education and community care vocational education. For economic education this is quite remarkable since a mismatch in educational level does not seem to have any impact on wages of school-leavers from this educational category. Moreover, economics is generally thought to be less occupation-specific than technical or agricultural vocational education. For school-leavers of community care vocational education the wage loss when their educational branch does not match with their job is considerable, at about 13%.

From the regression results we can conclude that mismatches with respect to level of education do indeed lead to lower earnings for school-leavers from technical and community care vocational education. School-leavers from agricultural vocational education do not earn less when working in a job on a lower level than their actual educational level. School-leavers from economic and business administration vocational education only earn less if they are working in a job that does not match with respect to branch. Mismatches by branch also negatively affect earnings from community care vocational education but have no significant effect on wages for school-leavers from agricultural or technical vocational education.

Finally, we want to examine the effect of educational mismatches on the probability of earning a low wage. Therefore we estimated a Logit model of which the results are presented in Table 9.7. In this model we have included dummy variables, for the acquired level of education and for mismatches with respect to level and branch. All other explanatory variables in the analysis are the same as the variables in the wage regressions. The table shows that women have a significantly higher chance of receiving a low wage for agricultural and technical vocational education only. Women that have attended community care education have a smaller chance of a low wage than men. Age only has a negative impact on the probability of low pay for school-leavers from economic and community care vocational education. Ethnic minorities never have a significant higher probability of low-wage employment.

Organizational characteristics do affect the probability of receiving a low wage. This probability decreases with firm size for school-leavers from agricultural and economic vocational education.[7] Working in a profit organization only significantly increases the probability of low pay for school-leavers from community care vocational education. Contrary to what Table 9.3 suggested, it appears that once we correct for other factors, school-leavers of Intermediate Vocational Education have the highest relative probability of a low wage for all educational sectors distinguished. Investing in Intermediate Vocational Education is more risky than investing in Preparatory or short-Intermediate Vocational Education. As expected, overschooling leads to a higher chance of a low wage for school-leavers of technical and community care vocational education but not for school-leavers from agricultural and economic education. Underschooling only has a significant influence on the probability of a low wage for school-leavers of economic vocational education. Mismatches with respect to level do not affect the probability of a low wage for school-leavers from agricultural

Table 9.7:

Logit analysis of the probability of a low wage by branch of study

	Agriculture	Technical	Economics	Community care
Educational level of school-leaver:				
PVE	Reference	Reference	Reference	Reference
Short IVE	0.539	1.155	2.471	1.435
	(0.17)	**(3.86)	**(6.41)	(2.09)
IVE	3.687	2.747	4.418	2.956
	**(14.30)	**(15.86)	**(19.48)	**(17.11)
Match:				
Overschooling	0.359	1.137	0.214	1.093
(dummy)	(1.10)	**(16.16)	(0.45)	**(13.95)
Underschooling	1.332	0.276	1.951	-3.846
(dummy)	(1.91)	(0.22)	**(7.16)	(0.16)
Mismatch by	0.242	0.298	0.489	1.375
branch	(0.51)	(1.25)	(2.10)	**(19.85)
Undertaking	0.249	0.398	-0.177	0.402
apprenticeship	(0.19)	(1.25)	(0.45)	(1.22)
Personal characteristics:				
Age	-2.534	-0.917	-6.422	-1.562
	(2.62)	(0.39)	**(21.69)	**(23.32)
Age squared	0.046	0.004	0.134	0.025
	(1.49)	(0.01)	**(17.46)	**(22.18)
Female	1.349	0.549	-0.062	-0.955
	**(19.43)	*(3.74)	(0.04)	**(4.23)
Ethnic minority	-2.817	0.846	0.530	-1.033
	(0.02)	(1.50)	(0.48)	(0.92)
Organizational characteristics:				
Firm size				
< 10 workers	Reference	Reference	Reference	Reference
10–99 workers	-0.167	-0.294	-0.663	0.108
	(0.28)	(0.87)	*(3.32)	(0.10)
100–499 workers	-1.237	-0.326	-0.332	-0.129
	*(3.40)	(0.61)	(0.45)	(0.09)
>500 workers	-2.087	-0.111	-0.433	0.208
	**(3.94)	(0.09)	(1.24)	(0.32)
Profit organization	0.454	-0.254	0.602	0.547
	(0.99)	(0.37)	(0.91)	*(2.84)
Constant	26.287	12.202	67.378	15.552
	*(2.75)	(0.69)	**(22.52)	**(14.30)

* significant at 10%-level; ** significant at 5%-level; (Wald-test in brackets)

education. Finally, a mismatch by branch of study only leads to a higher probability of a low wage for school-leavers of community care vocationa education. Since this is a labour market segment with strict regulations and therefore one-to-one relationships between education and work this result is not unsurprising.

5   CONCLUSIONS

In this chapter we have examined the low wages of school-leavers in the Netherlands and especially the relation between low wages and mismatches between education and occupation. We may conclude that in general it does matter for wages whether the job a school-leaver has obtained matches his or her educational level. The match between the branch of study and the branch of the job seems to be less relevant: only for economics and business administration and for the community care sector are significant effects on the wages found. As a consequence mismatches also affect the probability of a low wage. Table 9.8 shows the simulated effects of mismatches between education and work. The reference in this table is a school-leaver from Intermediate Vocational Education, 20 years old, male, native, not on an apprenticeship programme, and working in a small non-profit organization. Furthermore this reference school-leaver has a job that matches his education with respect to both level and education.

Table 9.8:

The probability of a low wage by branch of study

Differences in percentage points compared to reference (simulated effects)

	Agriculture	Technical	Economics	Community care
Reference	9.1%	14.3%	4.5%	6.1%
Overschooling	+3.4	+19.9**	+1.1	+10.2**
Underschooling	+18.3	+3.7	+20.6**	−6.0
Mismatch by branch	+2.2	+4.0	+2.7	+14.4**

** significant at the 5%-level

The table shows that for the reference school-leaver the risk of low-wage employment is highest for those that have completed a technical study. For those that have completed a study in economics and business administration this risk is very low. Although the effects of mismatches on the probability of earning a low wage is often not significantly different from zero, in cases where it is, the effect is very large. For example for school-leavers in economics and business education, underschooling increases the probability of low pay for the reference school-leavers from 4.5% to over 25%. Nevertheless mismatches only partly explain low-wage employment. Other factors, like personal characteristics that we do not observe, might be of more importance in explaining the probability of low-wage employment.

APPENDIX 9.A

Table 9.A.1:
Number of years per level of education

Educational level	Number of years
Primary education	6
Lower General Secondary Education/Preparatory Vocational Education	10
Short-Intermediate Vocational Education	12
Intermediate Vocational Education/Higher General Secondary Education	13
Higher Vocational Education/University Education	16

NOTES

1. But may also occur in a later stadium of the career, for example after a job loss.
2. See also Arents, Heijke, and Koeslag (1996) for an application with respect to economists at University level and Higher Vocational Education level.
3. The job matching theory does, however, not explain why mismatches occur and why only some individuals are confronted with mismatches while others are not.
4. RUBS is an abbreviation in Dutch: 'Registratie van Bestemming en Uitstroom van Schoolverlaters', translated as Registration of the Destination and Outflow of School-leavers.
5. People, who are not risk-neutral, will also consider the variance in earnings, i.e. the risk of having a much lower wage than the median. In that situation a higher probability on a low wage for a specific type of education, at a given median wage, will lead to less investment in that type of education.
6. For measuring the worker's job level, we have used the self-assessment method (see Hartog and Jonker, 1996). More precisely, in the questionnaire the individuals are asked to identify the educational requirements for their jobs according to their employers. Furthermore people are asked what branch of study was required according to their employers.
7. Recently, similar results have been found by Van Praag and Oosterbeek (1993

REFERENCES

Arents, M., H. Heijke, M. Koeslag (1996), *A comparison of the labour market position of university education and higher vocational education in economics and business administration*, ROA-RM-1996/1E, Maastricht.

Becker, G.S. (1962), *'Investment in human capital: a theoretical analysis'*, Journal of Political Economy, **70**, 9–49.

CBS (1991), Sociaal-economisch panelonderzoek. Inhoud, opzet en organisatie (Socio-economic panel research. Contents, structure, and organisation), CBS, Voorburg/Heerlen.

Cohn, E. and Kahn, S.P. (1995), *'The wage effect of overschooling revisited'*, Labour Economics, **2**, 67–76.

Hartog, J. (1992), *Capabilities, allocation and earnings*, Kluwer Academic Publishers, Boston/Dordrecht/London.

Hartog, J. and Jonker, N. (1996), A job to match your education: does it matter?, Paper presented at ROA-10, Maastricht, 6–7 June.

Hartog, J. and Oosterbeek, H. (1988), 'Education, allocation and earnings in the Netherlands', Economics of Education Review, **7**, 185–194.

Hirschleifer, J. (1973), Where are we in the theory of information?, American Economic Review, **63**, 31–39.

Schultz, T.W. (1961), 'Investment in human capital', American Economic Review, **51**, 1–17.

Thurow, L. (1979), *'A job competition model'*, in M. Piore (ed.), Unemployment and inflation; institutionalist and structuralist views, White Plains, New York.

Van Praag, C.M., H. Oosterbeek (1993). Anomalie: grotere bedrijven betalen hogere lonen (Anomaly: larger firms pay higher wages), Economisch Statistische Berichten, **78**, 764–768.

Van Smoorenburg, M.S.M., E.J.T.A. Willems (1996), *Schoolverlaters tussen onderwijs en arbeidsmarkt 1995* (School-leavers between education and the labour market 1995), ROA-R-1996/3, Maastricht.

Index

DATE DUE

OCT 04 1999

RETURNED
APR 1 5 2000

THE LIBRARY STORE   #47-0103 Pre-Gummed